ADVANCE PRAISE FOR RED COAT DIARIES

"In a time where police services across Canada are having difficulty recruiting women I found this book to be extremely motivating in promoting policing as a profession."
　　　　– Jennifer Evans, Chief of Police, Peel Regional Police

"I am very pleased to endorse *Red Coat Diaries: True Stories from the Women of the Royal Canadian Mounted Police* which continues to document the remarkable and very unique stories that our female members (and spouses) have experienced in the Force since 1974."
　　　　– Deputy Commissioner Marianne Ryan,
　　　　Commanding Officer, Alberta Canada

"*Red Coat Diaries: True Stories From The Women of the Royal Canadian Mounted Police* is a must read. It will make you proud to be Canadian."
　　　　– Ward Clapham, author,
　　　　Lead Big: Discovering the Upside of Unconventional Leadership

RED COAT DIARIES

TRUE STORIES
FROM THE WOMEN OF THE
ROYAL CANADIAN MOUNTED POLICE

Library and Archives Canada Cataloguing in Publication

Red coat diaries : true stories from the women of the RCMP / edited
by Aaron Sheedy, Regina Marini, Veronica Fox.

Issued in print and electronic formats.
ISBN 978-1-77161-153-4 (paperback).--ISBN 978-1-77161-154-1 (html).--
ISBN 978-1-77161-155-8 (pdf)

1. Royal Canadian Mounted Police--Anecdotes. 2. Policewomen--
Canada--Anecdotes. I. Sheedy, Aaron, 1973-, editor II. Marini, Regina,
1962-, editor III. Fox, Veronica, 1980-, editor

HV8158.7.R69R434 2015   363.20971   C2015-907073-2
                                                  C2015-907074-0

Pubished by Mosaic Press, Oakville, Ontario, Canada, 2015.
Distributed in the United States by Bookmasters (www.bookmasters.com).
Distributed in the U.K. by Roundhouse Group (https://www.roundhousegroup.co.uk).

MOSAIC PRESS, Publishers
Copyright © 2015 the authors

Printed and Bound in Canada.
Design and layout by Eric Normann/Keith Daniel

Cover photo by Saffron Blaze. Dowloaded from Wikimedia Commons and used under
Creative Commons license (https://commons.wikimedia.org/wiki/File:RCMP_Riders.jpg).
Photo modifications (cropping and blurring) by Eric Normann

We acknowledge the Ontario Media Development Corporation for their support of
our publishing program

We acknowledge the Ontario Arts Council for their support of our publishing program

ONTARIO ARTS COUNCIL
CONSEIL DES ARTS DE L'ONTARIO
an Ontario government agency
un organisme du gouvernement de l'Ontario

We acknowledge the financial support of
the Government of Canada through the
Canada Book Fund (CBF) for this project.

Nous reconnaissons l'aide financière du gouvernement du Canada par l'entremise du Fonds
du livre du Canada (FLC) pour ce projet.

Canadian   Patrimoine
Heritage   canadien

Canadä

MOSAIC PRESS
1252 Speers Road, Units 1 & 2
Oakville, Ontario L6L 5N9
phone: (905) 825-2130

info@mosaic-press.com

www.mosaic-press.com

RED COAT DIARIES

TRUE STORIES
FROM THE WOMEN OF THE
ROYAL CANADIAN MOUNTED POLICE

Edited by Aaron Sheedy, Veronica Fox
and Regina Marini

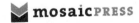
mosaicPRESS

In Memory of

Constable Della Beyak

Special Constable Nancy Puttkemery

Constable Christine Diotte

Constable Robin Cameron

Constable Chelsey Robinson

Your legacy and spirit lives on in the pages of this book.

Dedicated to

The women of Troop 17, whose courage and strength helped shape the Force as we know it today.

And to every member of the RCMP who supported diversity, in all its varied kinds, in the workplace.

Disclaimer

The stories contained in this book are true to life anecdotes. Events, locales and conversations have been recreated from the memories of the individual story contributors. In each story, the names of vulnerable persons have either been changed or omitted in order to maintain their anonymity and protect their privacy. In certain stories, some identifying characteristics, such as physical descriptions and places of residence, have also been changed or omitted. Any opinions or beliefs, either implied or expressed, are those of the individual contributor.

CONTENTS

Part III: Nowhere Near Ordinary

"You've come a long way, baby." This phrase, which some might consider to be politically incorrect, describes exactly how I feel when I think about my more than 40-year-long journey as one of the first female police officers in the RCMP.

This recent addition to the Red Coat Diaries series recognizes, celebrates and preserves some of the previously untold adventures and experiences of female members of the RCMP. Fellow members of Troop 17: This book is dedicated to us!

As I write this, we are celebrating the 40th anniversary of women serving as police officers in the RCMP. Back in 1974, who would have imagined that thirty-two young women from across Canada would later be called trailblazers or leaders? We just wanted to be called Mounties.

I recall the day I applied to the RCMP: May 23, 1974. While driving through Dartmouth, Nova Scotia, I heard a radio news broadcast reporting that the RCMP had just started accepting women as regular members of the Force. I happened to be driving past the local RCMP detachment and it felt like destiny was calling. I pulled into the detachment parking lot that morning and went inside to get an application.

I was greeted at the front counter by a young constable, who asked me how he could help. When I told him that I wanted to apply to become a police officer, he gave me a puzzled look and advised me that the Force did not accept women. Just then, another member entered the lobby through the back door. From the look on his face, it was obvious he'd heard the same news broadcast that I had. It seemed to me as if he knew that life in Canada (and maybe on this planet) as we all knew it, was about to change.

If that was indeed what he was thinking, history has clearly demonstrated that he was right.

That morning I got my application to become a regular member of the RCMP, and the rest, as they say, is history.

I have loved every minute of my career and the friends and adventures that came with it. Well, maybe not the 3:00 a.m. callouts, but most of it. And although I have never looked back, I have paused to reflect on my origins.

The story does not start with Troop 17. Women in Canada had been pushing the boundaries for some time. It was well into the 20th century before women were declared "persons" under the law and earned their right to vote. On a more personal level, my mother was one of many young women who joined the Canadian Armed Forces during World War II to help keep our country free, only to be told at the end of the war that her services were no longer required. My peers and I each had different influences in our lives that made the choice to join the RCMP seem like the right thing to do, or at least raised the question, "Why not be a Mountie?"

Although female police officers were not officially accepted into the RCMP until 1974, there were a number of female civilian employees who had previously served in traditional policing roles within the Force, including acting in undercover operations and guarding females lodged in cells. There was also a long tradition of the wives of regular members performing various police-related duties alongside their operational husbands. These women were essentially the unpaid "second man" in many remote postings and have been recognized only recently for their contribution to the RCMP's establishment across Canada. Today's women serving in all areas in the Force continue to embrace gender-related challenges with courage and class.

I have said in the past and continue to believe that every employee of the RCMP has the potential to write a bestseller about the danger, sacrifice, heroism and adventure that comes with the job. The stories contained in this book, whether they are told with drama, humour or a little of both, are a testament to the dedication, courage and sacrifice of our members.

I am so proud of each of my troop mates and those who have followed in our footsteps, some creating their own unique pathways. My own daughter now proudly serves among this next generation of women Mounties.

It has truly been a privilege to have been one of the first female police officers in the RCMP. I am also eternally grateful and incredibly proud to have had the opportunity to be a part of an organization made up of brave men and women who continue to serve our communities with honour and distinction.

Commissioner Bev Busson (Ret.)

ACKNOWLEDGMENTS

I am a feminist; at least when it comes to the Royal Canadian Mounted Police (RCMP). Change is afoot for the Mounties and as we evolve into the modern world I am convinced that Canadians and RCMP employees alike will be best served by continuing to actively increase the number of women being hired and women being promoted within our ranks. I want to see big changes in my RCMP and the easiest, most cost effective, legal and dramatic change we can make is to embrace diversity and raise up under-heard voices. If this scares anyone, if anyone believes that women aren't up for the job, you're holding proof to the contrary. Through these 40 stories everyone will see that women in the RCMP are brave, creative, natural trailblazers and most importantly they approach policing differently. In the story from this book, "No Prince Charming" Inspector Ruth Roy summed it up the best, "That summer I learned that I could never approach my work like one of the guys. I had to do police work my own way, a female way." I want to see what happens when the "female way" becomes mainstream.

In the way of gratitude, I would like to personally thank everyone who contributed writing to our little project. We'd be nowhere without you! Thank you so much. We are honoured to share your work.

As you might imagine there is a lot of work involved in a publication like this by many people. Our work-horse-in-chief was Veronica Fox. She signed on shortly after the first *Red Coat Diaries* and we started collecting stories for this book. Through thick and thin she was there as my partner in crime and my sounding board, she contributed stories, she recruited writers and did the lion's share of the content editing. Vee, simply, thank you. You got us to here!

Why be good when you can be great? Regina Marini has one of the strongest personal networks that I have ever seen and when she signed on to *Red Coat Diaries* doors opened for us. Her ability to end-run any number of problems, to recruit contributors and get us places we couldn't go ourselves has been invaluable. The stories in this book are great! Reg, thank you for helping us tell the world.

Red Coat Diaries enjoys a unique relationship with RCMP management. Time and time again we get support from within including from Strategic Partnerships and Heritage Branch and especially Spiro Hadjis, who reviewed this book for security issues. We get support from Corporate Communications and local, provincial and national RCMP Media Units. I am grateful also for the support from my coworkers and supervisors. Overall, the response is encouraging and a testament to the true Esprit de Corps that exists within the RCMP.

On the home front, I would like to thank the women I live with; my soon-to-be wife Carla Cormack and my step-daughter, Grace Manning. You are strong women and inspiration for the work I did on this book. I love you both.

I'd like to thank Howard Aster, Matthew Goody and everyone at Mosaic Press for their fearless support for the *Red Coat Diaries* series over the years. I would also like to recognize my friend Paul Shaughnessy for his professional insights and continued support .

Last and certainly not least, my parents and siblings. From them I have gleaned the right mix of creativity and hard work. Thank you.

Constable Aaron Sheedy
Toronto, Ontario

When I was around three years old, Mum introduced me to my first real book. Of course I'd had my share of baby picture books, but this one, she told me, was different: It had lots of words.

I eagerly flipped through, but with each turn of the page my anxiety mounted. What were all these symbols? I didn't understand any of it. Why wasn't this working? Mum noticed my mood and asked what was wrong.

"I can't read!" I cried.

"Oh, Veronica," she said. "Things don't happen that way. It takes time."

All those years ago, I'd never have imagined writing acknowledgements for a book. What a difference a few decades can make.

Many people have contributed to my personal and professional growth over the years. Starting from my days at Depot, the RCMP's training academy, I've been blessed to work for a number of forward-thinking managers, supervisors and mentors. Thank you all for encouraging my passion for the job, trusting me to lead and extending to me some amazing opportunities that have led me to where I am today.

To my troop mates, watch mates, colleagues, partners and peers: The past 10 years have flown. Thank you for being there during the often exciting, frequently fun, but sometimes quite difficult times. My close civilian friends also receive many thanks for being there through thick and thin. Thanks for embracing and celebrating my role as cop while keeping me grounded in the world outside of policing.

Writing is a deeply personal thing. To each contributor with whom I worked I say a heartfelt thank you for trusting me to touch your stories. Thanks as well to my co-editors Aaron and Regina and the people at Mosaic Press who've all contributed to bring this book and its stories to life.

To the women of Troop 17: Your courage, resolve and resilience was a game changer and has impacted me greatly. I thank and salute you.

My character is built, in part, on the generational grounding of my extended family. Both sides overcame many challenges so that my parents could be born in Canada, and I, in turn, could become a Mountie. Thank you for your legacy. And thanks to my relatives remaining today who help carry that legacy forward.

From my father I learned the value of hard work and commitment. I hear your words of wisdom daily: "Never lower your standards." Thanks,

Dad. My mother taught me the power of conviction and instilled in me a strong sense of social justice. I rely on these values every day. Thanks, Mum. And to Joshua, my dear brother: Your strength of character taught me to never give up no matter what challenges lie in the path. I miss you dearly and will never forget your smile. Until we meet again.

Corporal Veronica S.E. Fox
Port Coquitlam, British Columbia

Over the last few years of my 33 year career, I have had the great pleasure and honour of being involved in a number of great initiatives promoting women and diversity within the RCMP. From my involvement with the Ontario Women in Law Enforcement organization, teaching Diversity at Georgian College or participation internally on many RCMP committees, the question consistently received from the general public was, "What is it was really like to be a women in the RCMP?" Joining forces with Aaron Sheedy and Veronica Fox we embarked on a literary journey to seek out stories from across Canada from female RCMP employees. Who better to hear from than the ladies themselves about how they proactively overcame challenges, changed popular or traditional beliefs, garnered respect from their colleagues and ultimately changed the face of policing. It was our great honour to bring a "voice" to the women of the Royal Canadian Mounted Police.

No great journey happens without the support of those around us. First and foremost, I want to thank the contributors as without their contributions, this book would not have been possible. Their fearlessness demonstrates the "right stuff" and together their "voices" celebrate the indomitable spirit that defines what it truly means to be a woman in the Royal Canadian Mounted Police.

To the courageous women of Troop 17, who demonstrated fortitude and courage nowhere near ordinary and blazed a trail for the ladies that followed. We salute you!

To the visionary leadership within the RCMP, Peel Regional Police Service, Ottawa Police Service and Ontario Provincial Police who have supported and or endorsed the publication of this book. Sincere thanks go to Retired RCMP Commissioner Bev Busson, RCMP Deputy Commissioners Marianne Ryan and Peter Henschel, RCMP Chief Superintendent Jennifer Strachan, RCMP Director General Shirley Cuillierrier, Retired Ontario Provincial Police Commissioner Gwen Boniface, RCMP Chief Superintendent Marlene Snowman, Ottawa Police service Acting Chief Jill Skinner, Peel Regional Police Service Chief Jennifer Evans, Retired RCMP Inspector Elder Jim Potts and RCMP Superintendents Shahin Mezdizadeh and Robert Davis. Last but certainly not least: RCMP Manager Diversity and Employment Equity Ms. Janet Henstock.

To our publisher Mosaic Press, thank you for your vision and expertise to make this book a reality.

To all those at my first Detachment in Falcon Lake, Manitoba, who welcomed a young recruit and accepted, supported, guided, extended friendship and enriched my early career and life in so many positive ways: Special thanks go to Larry, Ernie, John, Jim, Rick, Serge, Erika, Evelyn, Sue, Don, Doug, Wendy, Judy, Shirley, and Bob. You will never be forgotten.

To my mother, I thank for passing on her indomitable spirit. To my father, I thank for his military discipline and stubbornness that prepared and equipped me to meet the challenges of a career nowhere near ordinary. To my sister, I thank for her ongoing love, strength and loving family.

To my very large RCMP family, and you know who you are, that through my long career, supported, extended friendship, demonstrated forward thinking, were non-judgmental, were open to change, walked the talk, were flexible, provided mentorship, guidance, opportunities, recognition, acceptance: please accept my sincere thanks. Like many families, it is the ones who did the complete opposite that I must especially thank for it tested and expanded my resolve, strengthened the content of my character, expanded my compassion and empathy for others, especially those in need, and inspired the development of leadership traits so critical to policing. To them, I am truly indebted. As I near the end of my career I salute my RCMP family and pass the torch. Your sacrifices, commitment and courage in the face of life threatening perils will forever be etched on my soul with the upmost pride.

And to the five women who exemplified that spirit and gave the ultimate sacrifice and lost their lives in the line of duty: Constable Della Beyak, Special Constable Nancy Puttkemery, Constable Christine Diotte, Constable Robin Cameron, Constable Chelsey Robinson; Your legacy and spirit lives on in the pages of this book.

Last, but certainly not least, heartfelt thanks to my forward thinking husband Daniel and two sons, Conor and Brandan, who listened, understood my commitment, inspired, loved unconditionally and encouraged me on those "good" days and "bad" days and will forever remain champions of my heart.

To my RCMP sisters and brothers, I salute you and part with Mahatma Gandhi's inspirational message: "Be the change you wish to see in the world."

Sergeant Regina A. Marini
Toronto, Ontario

PART I

BREAKING GROUND

BATHTUBS AND BATONS
Constable Connie Pinnegar, née Smith (Ret.)

The members of Troop 17 (the first troop of women in the RCMP) received the theory portion of riot training only. We did not get any hands-on instruction. We were told that women did not have the size to be an effective presence on a riot squad and would therefore never be asked to participate in this duty.

When I graduated from Depot, I went off to my first posting in Nanaimo, British Columbia, which is centrally located on Vancouver Island. Nanaimo is the host community for the annual World Championship Bathtub Race. The race was originally a 36 mile course from Nanaimo to Vancouver's English Bay across the Strait of Georgia. While the course has changed over the years, the concept has remained the same. Each participant races in a fibreglass bathtub mounted on a high speed boat hull, powered by a single eight horsepower engine. Prizes are simple trophies and bragging rights. Each July, people from all over the world descend on the city to take part in the festival and race. That's why Nanaimo claims the title as the Bathtub Racing Capital of the World. But my first summer in Nanaimo, the city got another name: Home of the 1975 Bathtub Weekend Riot.

One evening during the weekend festivities, a number of other members and I were on foot patrol in Nanaimo's downtown core. Things were heating up with the usual revellers and party-goers, but as the evening progressed the celebratory mood began to change. Suddenly, someone smashed a liquor store window and a group began ransacking the store. A dangerous mob mentality began to spread through the crowd.

Those of us assigned to foot patrol in the downtown core were called back to the office. Six of us managed to squeeze into a patrol car near the Bastion, a local landmark on the Nanaimo waterfront. Just as we closed the doors, the crowd, now in a frenzy, swarmed over our vehicle, smashing and rocking it. We were fortunate that our driver was able to ease us out of the rioting mass of people.

Back at the detachment, they were handing out riot gear.

Sergeant Al "Grizzly" Rivers stood in front of me holding an armful of equipment and growled, "Well, do you want it?"

Obviously he had not talked to anyone at Depot, but I like to think that I had proven my worth as a police officer.

As is my nature, there was no hesitation. I grabbed the gear and tried to hide a smile as I turned away, adrenaline pumping through my veins.

The riot line set up across the main street in the downtown core. As I held my position in the line, I mentally prepared myself by recalling the theory I had learned at Depot. Do not interact with the crowd. Do not react until told. Stand your ground. Everything was going well until a man in the crowd recognized who I was, despite being hidden behind a helmet and shield. I was Nanaimo's first and only female member of the RCMP at the time. He got right in my face, creating a scene and causing further disruption.

I thought, *My presence is causing a problem. I need to take care of this.*

I placed my hands on either end of my baton and held it horizontally at chest level. I slowly straightened my arms, touching the baton to his chest and in a low voice calmly said, "Stay back."

He took a step back and I had no further trouble with him. But, that was by no means the end of the riot. By the following morning, our cell block was full to overflowing, and we had prisoners lined up on the street outside waiting to be processed.

A few days later, my father, a commercial fisherman, delivered a load of salmon to Port Alberni, a town on the west coast of Vancouver Island, about 85 kilometres northwest of Nanaimo. As he walked up the dock, he overheard a group of fishermen on the deck of their boat, discussing their weekend plans. There was talk of going into Nanaimo to party and spend some hard-earned cash.

"If you're planning to party in Nanaimo, watch out for that female cop," warned one fisherman.

My father just smiled and carried on.

I later learned that the story going around about the incident with the man on the riot line had taken on a life of its own. Apparently I'd driven my baton into his gut, laying him out cold on the street.

I had developed quite a reputation. I have to say it served me well. I never again had any real trouble on the streets of Nanaimo. I was only met with respect.

A MOUNTIE'S ITALIAN CONNECTION
Sergeant Regina A. Marini

One spring morning in 1997, I arrived to work at the RCMP's Toronto-based Proceeds of Crime Unit to find I was now in charge of a high profile and complex international drug importation case. Two of the lead crime investigators on the project had suddenly retired, leaving me as the only investigator on the team with enough requisite knowledge to continue the investigation. My boss assigned me to be the lead investigator; it was the most daunting and yet exciting thing that could have ever happened to me.

We had been investigating a group of individuals with links to the Italian Mafia for some time. Historical police intelligence information gathered from various places including Montreal, England, Venezuela, Switzerland and Italy confirmed that this group was very active in the international drug importation business. Newer intelligence revealed that they had taken up primary residency in Canada, practically at our back door. In fact, the kingpin of this illegal organization was actually living in Toronto.

My team worked with the RCMP Combined Forces Special Enforcement Unit and authorities in the United States, Italy and South America. Our collective goal was to bring this group's illegal drug importation activities to an end. We were hot on their trail.

Things heated up when the "Toronto Kingpin" was tried and convicted *in absentia* of international drug trafficking by the Italian judicial authorities. On our end, we needed to prove that the Toronto Kingpin's extravagant Canadian lifestyle had been derived from his criminal activities; that his multiple mansions, luxury cars, frequent and expensive vacations, opulent jewelry and all other publicly displayed indications of wealth were proceeds of crime.

To prove our case, we needed the same hard evidence that had convinced the Italian judicial authorities of the Toronto Kingpin's criminality. As a result, my policing journey took a surreal turn. I found myself booking a flight to Italy. I'd never visited the land of my cultural heritage before, so I was understandably excited. Being first-generation Canadian, I had often heard stories from my parents about my Italian roots in Perugia, just north of Rome, but never dreamed that I would get to go to Italy. I was to travel with a member of the Canadian Federal Crown Counsel and another member from the Proceeds of Crime Unit who was fluent in Italian. Trips overseas such as this were a fairly rare occurrence so there was a lot of buzz generated in the office. When people realized that the three of us travelling to Italy all happened to be women, we became the butt of a number of "shoe shopping expedition" jokes. I was determined to turn such comments on their heads, but little did I know the significance our journey was really going to take.

With my first son only ten months old, and best wishes from my supportive husband, I packed my bags for a trip I thought would only last a few days. The ten hour flight to Rome was long, but our greeting by the RCMP liaison officer was most welcoming. He met us at the airport and took us to our hotel in the centre of the city.

Rome was beyond my wildest dreams. It was such a beautiful city, full of rich history, sunshine, ancient buildings and people in a hurry. Traffic was crazy. There did not appear to be any designated lanes. Instead, cars squeezed and merged wherever they could while Vespa weaved in and out of traffic and often up onto the sidewalk.

"Hey!" I pointed out the window. "They are going through a red light!"

I was told that traffic lights were more of a suggestion rather than a rule.

I was very happy to let someone else do the driving. After arriving gratefully in one piece at our hotel, we settled in for the night. In the morning, we had an important meeting with the Italian Police or *Carabinieri*.

In the morning, we met with a member of the Carabinieri who listened very intently as we briefed him on our case and explained what we were looking for and needed from the Italian courts. He told us that we should speak with his supervisor. The next morning, we met with the supervisor. He listened very intently as we briefed him on our case and explained what we were looking for and needed from the Italian courts. He told us that we should speak with the judicial magistrate for Mafia investigations in Rome.

The third morning we set out to meet with the judicial magistrate. This time, however, we were escorted in a police motorcade with sirens blaring as we roared through the streets of Rome. We travelled at a very high rate of speed towards the courthouse, weaving through heavy traffic, flying down narrow cobblestone streets and not stopping for any reason. My colleagues and I were squeezed into the backseat of a tiny European police car. Between the noise of the sirens and the bouncing of the vehicle, I started to feel a little queasy. I opened the window only to take in a lungful of thick exhaust fumes from a passing bus. I quickly rolled up the window and just held on. My companions and I could only laugh amongst ourselves at the attention we were getting from bystanders and motorists. Goodness knows what they must have been thinking.

We met with the lead magistrate for Mafia investigations only to have to schedule yet another meeting. But this time, we would be meeting with the highest ranking officer in the Carabinieri: the commander.

The meeting with the commander took place at a local restaurant, which to our surprise, had been closed to the public to allow for our exclusive use. The commander arrived with his entourage, while personnel were left outside to guard the cars. Security was extremely tight. At the time, the Carabinieri had been the target of violence perpetrated by the Mafia. As we learned, Carabinieri officers had been targeted and violently killed in several bomb attacks over the course of the past nine years. The violence perpetrated by the Mafia extended beyond the Carabinieri and had international implications. The commander filled us in on some of the history. In May, 1992, the Mafia assassinated the legendary prosecutor Judge Falcone, with a motorway bomb in Palermo, Sicily. Judge Falcone's wife and three bodyguards were also killed in the blast. Less than two months later, Judge Falcone's friend and colleague, Judge Borsellino, was also killed in Palermo when a car bomb went off outside his mother's home. These two incidents forever changed how many in Italy viewed the Mafia and the increased police scrutiny resulting from the murders caused many members of the Mafia to flee the country and seek refuge in other parts of the world. Canada was one of their chosen destinations.

The commander was willing to help us with our investigation in Canada as he recognized it could help bring an end to some of the violence in his own community in Italy. He agreed to make arrangements for us to pick up the evidence we required from the Palermo courts. We'd be making a side-trip to Sicily.

Having cleared up the formalities, the conversation shifted and the commander began asking us about how we as women had come to serve as police officers. He explained that there were no women in the Carabinieri, primarily due to a lack of proper facilities and training programs. The commander asked us about how the RCMP trained its women. We assured him that in the RCMP, women trained with men and worked in the same facilities without any problems. The commander seemed surprised and wanted to know if we were given five days off per month due to our "woman's cycle." We assured him that women worked regardless of where they were on "their cycle," performing the very same duties as men. The commander asked how long we had served in the RCMP. I told him that I had fifteen years on the job but that the RCMP had actually hired their first women in 1974. The commander was pleasantly surprised to hear this.

"It appears women are very capable investigators," he said.

The next day, our group of three flew to Palermo. Our short flight was uneventful until we approached the small island and were greeted by ominous-looking black clouds. The plane began to bounce around in the turbulence and the pilot announced that he had try to land at the airport. As we circled, we came very low to the sea. The wing of the plane appeared to be nearly touching the water. The runway jutted out from high cliffs. If the pilot did not make the runway, I was sure we'd have the sea or cliffs to greet us. My colleague did not want to look out the window and asked me to tell her when we were on the runway. We swayed from side to side as we came in for the landing. We were just about to touch down when all of a sudden the plane began to gain altitude. The pilot advised us that he was going to try again. I must say, I was not too keen on that because the storm was getting worse.

The plane circled several times before the pilot advised us that he had decided to land at the Catania Airport. Thank goodness. It was not until we were safe on the ground that we learned what we had tried to land in on the other side of the island. It turned out that the storm was the worst hurricane to hit Palermo in fifty years.

We spent several hours at the crowded Catania Airport, waiting for the storm to pass before boarding the same plane and returning to our intended destination. Thankfully, the storm had ended, but we arrived in Palermo to find uprooted palm trees, overturned cars and debris all over the place.

We were greeted by a police captain who drove us to our hotel. On the way, he pointed out the crater at the side of the road which still remained from the murder of Judge Falcone.

At our hotel, the police captain introduced us to the security detail that would remain outside our hotel all day and night. We were quite astounded with the security. Before departing, the captain announced he would pick us up in the morning and take us to meet his commander.

The next morning was gloriously beautiful when, as promised, the police captain arrived at our hotel. But despite the sunshine, the atmosphere in the vehicle turned ominous when the police captain stopped the car at a roadside monument that had been erected for Judge Falcone and his wife near their former home. Fresh flowers were laid at its base as if the murders had happened only yesterday. It was obviously quite a poignant incident that was still fresh in the minds of local citizens.

"To this day, the many Mafia families instigate a lot of violence amongst each other for control of illegal activities," the police captain told us. "They also target the police and judicial officials."

Turning from the monument, the police captain scanned the horizon.

"The police always have to be vigilant about being followed. We are careful not to lead enemies to our families."

We followed the police captain to our waiting vehicle sobered by the realization of just how dangerous it was to be a police officer or judicial official in Italy.

When we walked into the headquarters of the Palermo based Carabinieri Police, a number of male officers came out of their offices to watch us pass by. The police captain explained that word of the visiting women police officers from Canada had quickly spread through their headquarters.

"They have never seen women police officers before, so you are quite unique," he said.

The police captain introduced us to his commander who met with us briefly before personally escorting us to the Palermo Courthouse. We travelled the streets of Palermo in his motorcade, police sirens blaring all the way to the courthouse.

The courthouse was like an armed camp. The perimeter was protected by barbed wire-topped fencing and snipers. Guards at the front gate used mirrors to inspect the undercarriages of each motorcade vehicle. Even the commander himself handed over identification and paperwork for scrutiny.

Once inside the perimeter, we exited the vehicles and were escorted through a series of metal detectors. We learned that all court officials, lawyers, magistrates and even judges underwent the same process every day they came to work. The murders of Judges Falcone and Borsellino had left an everlasting legacy.

We were escorted to an office where a court clerk handed us an official-looking package bearing all the court seals and notarizations needed to ensure admissibility to court proceedings in Canada. And just like that, we had what we needed. After all we'd been through, it seemed almost too easy. We'd expected that we'd need to spend countless hours searching on our own through court records for the documents we needed. We poured through the documents and confirmed everything was there, expressing our gratitude to the commander and court officials for supporting our investigation.

We three ladies returned to Canada a few days later, never to forget the courage, professionalism and hospitality of the Carabinieri. The evidence we obtained in Italy was integral to the successful prosecution of several Mafia leaders in Canada, including our very own Toronto Kingpin. And we did it all while resisting our "natural instinct" to shop for shoes! So much for stereotypes.

When I started my career during the early '80s in rural Manitoba I never imagined that I would someday have the opportunity to represent the RCMP (and women police officers in general) in the very country my family had originated from. But what really stands out was the day I picked up a long-distance phone call from that RCMP liaison officer who had met us in Rome.

"You're never going to believe this," he said. "The Carabinieri has announced in the Italian paper today that they've hired their first women police officers!"

EMERGENCY RESPONSE TEAM
Sergeant Valerie Brooks

I could hear their footsteps on the other side of the truck as they unloaded the bags of fertilizer and put them in the storage unit. We were in tight. This was happening now. This was the "Toronto 18" investigation. A million man-hours, not to mention millions of dollars, had been spent. Multiple policing and intelligence agencies were involved. The investigation into the eighteen Canadians who had been planning a domestic terror event had been thorough. Those sacks of fertilizer were ammonium nitrate, a compound that can be used as an explosive; those guys were suspected of being terrorists with the intention of causing harm to Canadians.

Most criminals regret earning the attention of the RCMP Emergency Response Team (ERT). That day, I was the "head of the stack," the lead "Assaulter," the person, the woman, who would come face-to-face with those criminals and bring their world crashing down on them. Amidst the intense focus and adrenaline coursing through my veins there was time for a small grin under my helmet and balaclava. I gripped my MP5 assault rifle and dug my boot into the pavement for traction. I'd earned my way here. I could hear my ERT-mates crashing through the front door. It was go time.

The Emergency Response Team is an elite team of specially trained police officers who are highly skilled in the job of entering and clearing areas that are deemed too dangerous for the everyday police officer. There are some specializations within ERT, like sniper or marine operator, but we are all Assaulters trained to take and keep the upper hand in potentially violent policing situations.

I had known that I wanted to get into the ERT Program in 1996 when I was an applicant waiting to get into the Force. During one of several ride-a-longs with various members at my local detachment I had had the opportunity to speak extensively with an ERT member. I was taken by his stories of the calls, the nature of the work, the training and the skill set required. I remember it like it was yesterday because it was a life turning point. I said that I wanted to be ERT and he responded by flatly telling me that women could not do the job of ERT. He was not overly arrogant, or trying to be mean. It was a long held perception that women could not handle the physical requirements of being on ERT and no woman had ever been on the team. He told me that unless I could pick up a two-hundred pound man and carry him twenty-five yards, I would not pass the ERT course, as this was a requirement.

Challenge accepted!

This discussion served as a catalyst. I was also drawn to the ERT program because of the various skill sets required to join the team. It required proficiency with weapons, an ability to repel and a high level of fitness combined with a degree of athleticism. Having grown up playing all sorts of team sports, including varsity basketball, I knew that I had the athletic ability and I enjoyed team environments and the camaraderie associated with team activities. The fact that this was an "elite" specialized team within the RCMP, and one in which no other female had ever been a part of in an operational capacity, made me want it even more.

Fast forward the story to the spring of 2002. I'd spent two years of General Duty policing in British Columbia and three years in Federal Policing in Ontario. There was an internal posting calling for interested members to try out for ERT. Doubt crept in right away. Did I want to put myself out there? Would I be accepted by the ERT members in Ontario? What would the reactions be nationally? I questioned if I was physically ready. The try-out was in just a few weeks. My supervisor was on ERT in Ontario and my husband was both ERT and part of the Special Emergency Response Team (SERT), which was a tactical counter-terrorism team. These men supported me in my quest to become an ERT member. I never thought that it would take nerve to send an email, but I mustered the courage to start on this path. I emailed my intention to try out.

From that point on, I was fully committed. I stepped up my training regiment and really began to focus on preparing for the ERT physical standards. I would need to successfully meet these on the morning of the selection course or I would be given no further consideration. The National ERT physical standards consisted of:

1 ½ miles in 11 minutes or less
40 continuous push ups

40 sit ups in a minute
5 pull ups
A single 145 pound bench press

These tasks had to be done with little rest in-between. Think it is easy? Try it. If you can do it with no problem, join the RCMP. We're hiring! And sign up for ERT. In fact, everyone struggles with the physical standard in some way. If you can bench a truck, you probably aren't a sprinter and that run will burn. For me, it was the bench press. I was 135 pounds at the time, so I had to bench press over my body weight.

The selection course is not just about finding individuals who can pass the physical standards. It is largely about identifying suitable potential candidates for the ERT Program as a whole. That is, identifying those with the aptitude to master the various specialized skill sets combined with the appropriate interpersonal skills to flourish in a team environment.

The path to ERT is as follows: You show your interest and get the support of your supervisors; from there, you get called to the Ontario Selection which starts with the physical standards test listed above. But passing that is just the start. If you pass Ontario Selection, you are brought on as a "Striker," sort of an "ERT-in-waiting." You attend training, but you can't go on operational call-outs. To earn that privilege, you must pass the National ERT Course. All that seemed like a lifetime away as I arrived for the Ontario Selection Course.

Every Ontario ERT member can recount the feeling they had arriving for the Ontario Selection. I was really, really nervous about performing the physical standards, most specifically my nemesis: the bench press. It was a lot of weight for me to press. My form needed to be perfect and I had not had much time to prepare. The first morning of the Ontario Selection, as promised, we started with the physical standards testing right off the hop. The run: simple. The sit-ups: please. The arm muscle activities of the pull-ups and pushups were challenging but accomplished with confidence. I was more worried about what toll they would take on the impending weight test. Everything could be all over with a single failed bench press. When it came to my turn at the bench, I was so jacked up with adrenalin that I could have benched a Shetland pony. Much to my surprise, and I think to the surprise of those gathered around to watch, I lifted the bar and completed one full rep without major difficulty. What a huge relief. But it was short-lived as we started our commute to a military base where we begin a four day test of our teamwork and shooting ability, and a demonstration of our motivation and desire (a.k.a. "grit"). Ask anyone who has been there: It is hell.

The next several days consisted of constant physical exertion including "fun runs," which took place morning, noon and in the middle of the night. I recall being rudely awakened to the sounds of garbage cans in the hallway being kicked over at around 2:00 a.m. after just having crawled into bed. We were ordered to assemble in 60 seconds on the parade square wearing gym attire ready for a lustrous midnight fun run which was really *not* fun. We also spent lots of time at the shooting range learning to use various weapons, practicing hands-on combat techniques, rappelling, doing bush tracks and orienteering, and disassembling, cleaning and reassembling weapons.

During a grappling session, where the goal was to pin your opponent but not get pinned yourself, I was matched against a two-hundred pound candidate. My goal was to not get pinned as pinning him didn't seem to be in the cards. At one point, as I pushed against the mat to squirm out from below, I heard and felt a pop in the ring finger of my left hand. In fact, everyone heard it and the action stopped. My finger was severely deformed and resembled a road map of the Rockies. I was devastated. Not only was I in extreme pain, but more importantly, I was terrified that I was not going to be able to complete the selection course. I had already endured two days of hell and had made it too far to turn back.

I was off to the hospital for a quick sniff of laughing gas and a sharp yank on my finger to relocate everything. I was discharged with a swollen, tender finger encased in a metal brace. Fortunately, the dislocation occurred on my left hand. Had it been my right hand, I would not have been able to hold a gun to shoot and would have been sent home. But with my left hand as my "support" hand, I was still able to fire a weapon and, thankfully, I was allowed to stay on the selection course. As if the selection course wasn't tough enough, now I was labouring with a tender finger and required to do literally everything with my right hand. Even simple things like dropping to the ground to do pushups was excruciating with my throbbing swollen finger.

We were all becoming physically and mentally drained. On the final day of the course, following a long, drawn-out shooting session at the range, we were informed that we would be running back to the base instead of driving back in the comfort of the vehicles we'd arrived in. This was the final test: A three mile run back to the base. To make things "interesting," we were collectively required to carry a number of items with us. These items consisted of a large two-man ram, a cooler full of ice water and one roll of Dixie cups. Off we went: The five of us running down the gravel road, working as a team and trying to share the workload. I could carry the ram only with my right hand while everyone else was able to alternate as fatigue in their arm set in. I believe this is where I lost two toenails (one on each foot) due to the distance that we were running in combat boots.

The final phase of the selection course was an individual candidate interview conducted by ERT members. The team members were given the opportunity to ask any questions they felt were necessary to determine a candidate's suitability for the team. Following this interview, the team held a vote (in private) to decide if the candidate would be invited to serve on the team as a Striker. In essence, it was a vote of acceptance by the established team as well as an agreement or pledge that they saw potential and would assist you in preparing for the National ERT Course.

I was accepted! I left that course a Striker, which was a role I stayed in for almost two years.

Preparing for the National ERT Course was a huge endeavour and something that I took very seriously. I held a strong belief that if you failed to prepare, you were prepared to fail. I did not like to fail. In terms of preparation, there was much to be done. For starters, I made a point of attending all of the team training days that I could possibly fit in. I knew that it was important to get as much exposure as possible to the numerous skill sets and tactics utilized by ERT. I knew that to successfully complete the National ERT Course I would have to qualify on three different weapons and pass an Assaulter Competency Test, among other things. For me, training days were also an opportunity to build rapport and continue the precarious process of earning the respect and confidence of the guys who would one day refer to me as their teammate.

Although the team was mandated to train at least two days of every month, I knew that this was not adequate and that extra preparation was necessary on my own time. Consequently, in the months leading up to the course, my husband and I spent many weekends in a gravel pit working on my shooting skills. As mentioned earlier, my husband played a huge role in helping me to prepare. He ran me through my paces, doing his best at creating an environment for me that simulated the actual course. This meant he was demanding and somewhat of a tyrant, not accepting anything less than 100 percent effort from me at all times.

In addition to shooting, I also spent time literally carrying my husband around. As it turned out, that particular "requirement" was a myth, but I still wanted to be prepared. I insisted that he show me the technique for a proper "fireman's carry." Basically, you reach down and grab one arm and one leg and then hoist them over your shoulder. We would be out walking our dogs in our neighbourhood and I would just throw him over my shoulder and continue on down the street. I'm sure the neighbours must have thought we were completely crazy! But later, during our first Fun Run on the National ERT Course we were required to stop running and pick up the person next to us. Of course, with my luck, I happened to be standing next to a strapping lad. But I had little difficulty picking him up and carrying him the required distance.

In addition to shooting, I dedicated countless hours to physical training. For me, a superior level of fitness was a must. Firstly, I had to avoid injuries. Any serious injury would preclude me from participating in qualifications and completing the course and I would be sent home. Second, I recognized that physical fitness, or "prowess," was the quickest way to earn respect and credibility in the ERT environment. Consequently, I hired an elite strength training coach, one who worked with Olympic athletes, and I embarked on a closely supervised and regimented power lifting program to get stronger and improve my overall fitness level. I set my goal at attaining an extremely high level of physical fitness. I was adamant that, as a woman, there was no room for mediocrity, especially since I was aspiring to be the first. I felt that in order to gain the respect of the ERT community, as a female, I could not be a marginal performer. In fact, I would have to be that much better in order to gain acceptance from even the harshest critics. Men might gain acceptance as marginal performers, but a women could not!

I spent almost two years as a Striker on the Ontario ERT team, with many of the guys serving as mentors along the way. In that time, I had the opportunity to earn the trust, respect and support from a few of team members who perhaps were not quite convinced that a woman had a place on an ERT team. Although no one ever discouraged me to my face, I was acutely aware that there were some naysayers out there. Regardless, I felt that I had demonstrated an aptitude as well as the work ethic and desire to succeed in the program. I genuinely felt like I had the "backing" of the Ontario team and on the day of my departure for the National ERT Course, all of them wished me luck, with many of them telling me to "go make them proud!"

I left home on a Sunday afternoon, bound for the National ERT Course in Ottawa. My car was loaded to the roof with equipment, tactical clothing and supplies for the coming weeks. Although I had waited almost two years for this opportunity, I was terrified as to how I would be received on the National Stage. Sure, I had ample time to demonstrate to the Ontario team that I was worthy of this opportunity, but what would those in Ottawa think? What would the instructors think? Would they be in favour? Would I be treated fairly or would there be efforts made to sabotage me? Also, the candidate pool would consist of twenty-seven guys from across the country. What would their attitudes be towards me? Would they be accepting and supportive? How would I be treated? It was a long drive alone with these thoughts from Milton to Ottawa.

All of these questions remained unanswered until the following morning which was Day One of the course. As candidates, we were told by the instructor cadre to assemble early in the morning in a gravel parking lot at Connaught Range to commence the ERT Physical Standards, beginning with the 1.5 mile run back to the gym. Those who were unsuccessful would be given a second opportunity on the following morning to complete the standards and if they failed again, they would be sent home. And that was the way it was. The threat of being sent home always loomed.

This time, I knew that I had arrived prepared and in peak condition to not just meet, but exceed the physical standards. The work was done and the physical standards wouldn't be an issue, but my goal was to "fit in" with the guys in every way possible. When it was time to test pull-ups, candidates proceeded individually while everyone else watched. I recall the first candidate in my group doing ten pull ups (the minimum requirement was five). The next candidate proceeded to do ten as well. The following three candidates did ten also. The "bar" had clearly been established at ten and it was obvious that everyone was counting. The sixth candidate struggled and managed only six pull-ups. When it was my turn, despite being physically capable of doing at least thirteen pull-ups, I chose to do ten. I had nothing to gain or prove by doing more. On the other hand, had I only been able to do five, the guys may have perceived me as weak or marginal from the onset. I believe to this day that my physical training and preparation earned me a degree of respect and acceptance very early on. This respect and acceptance grew as the course unfolded.

The National ERT Course is, in my opinion, by far the most difficult course delivered by the RCMP. In 2004, the course was five weeks in duration. Instruction was delivered for approximately thirteen hours per day and then there was time spent cleaning weapons and preparing and organizing gear for the following day. I believe we averaged about four hours of sleep most nights. Again, the concept is to wear candidates down physically and mentally to see if they are able to function and make sound decisions in a stressful environment. After all, this is the nature of the work. From a personal perspective, I felt immense pressure to succeed and to be the first female. Primarily this pressure was self-imposed. But there were all of those people who had invested time and energy into helping me along the way, including my husband and there were friends and family and colleagues back home rooting for me. I desperately did not want to disappoint them.

In terms of fitting in and gaining acceptance with the other candidates, this was not an issue. When you go through something as intense as the National ERT Course, you quickly learn to rely on each other as a survival mechanism and bonds quickly form. Everyone experiences failure in varying degrees on this course. Everyone has good days and bad days. I had my share of bad days and can honestly say that the support and encouragement that I received from the other candidates contributed significantly to my success on the course. Although what happens on the ERT course, stays on the ERT course, I can tell you that there was an event during a social night off base that made it crystal clear that they accepted me as one of their own, and that is all I will say except for it still makes me smile.

By the end of the course, over a third of the candidates had been sent home. It is a crazy hard course to pass for anyone. To date, passing the National ERT Course has been my biggest accomplishment from both a professional and personal perspective. I can say without hesitation that I was accepted into the ERT family.

And that was the path that brought me to the head of the stack behind that truck as I watched one of the suspects carry a sack of fertilizer into the storage unit. As I heard the entry being made at the front of the business we knew it was our cue to arrest the suspects in the back. They were not prepared and they did not stand a chance.

That is how it works: we prepare. Each of us has worked incredibly hard to be there and is one hundred percent focused and dedicated. We are a force to be reckoned with. On ERT, teamwork is not a boardroom concept, it is a real thing and it is as powerful as the ammunition in our weapons.

They were cuffed in seconds. They were not ready for us.

I spent four extremely enjoyable and rewarding years in ERT and participated in many call-outs, major events and summits. Many times I found myself in awe that people actually paid me to do such amazing work. The RCMP has a recruiting slogan: *A Career Nowhere Near Ordinary.* This really sums up working on ERT.

Along with the rewards, however, came considerable pressure and responsibility. The pressure came from being constantly watched and evaluated. Whether we were doing marine intervention, aircraft assault training or routine high-risk calls, I always felt like I was being assessed as a woman. The extra pressure forced me to bring my "A" game all the time, which is a good thing in ERT. But trust in ERT is extremely fragile. One mistake and it evaporates, probably forever. As the only female member, I never wanted to make a mistake as I knew it would serve as "proof" to those who still believed that a woman was not capable of doing the job.

I feel that one of the keys to my success in the ERT program was my prevailing attitude to do everything possible to blend in as a member of the team. From day one, it was always about the team and making the adjustment to having a female around as simple and minimally disruptive as possible for the guys. Although I had passed the National ERT Course and earned the right to be on the team, I was always mindful of the impact that my presence would have on the other twenty guys. My advice to other women who express an interest in the program is that you have to accept that it is a male dominated environment. If you are not comfortable with "guys being guys" from time to time, then ERT is not for you.

It took thirty years for a woman to serve as an operational ERT member and there has not been another woman since. This is surprising considering there are about 4000 female members in the RCMP. I do not know why women in ERT has not become a regular thing. It has been, to date, the most memorable four years of my career.

FROM CITY GIRL TO BUSH WOMAN
Sergeant Regina A. Marini

I arrived at my first posting in Falcon Lake, Manitoba one very cold February night in 1983. I was a city girl. I had just turned nineteen and grew up in some of the biggest cities in the world. The thought of living and working in a remote rural area with no friends or family nearby, and no amenities, brought an insecure reality to my new life. I had no idea of what to expect of life "in the bush" and I was even more anxious knowing that I was to be the only female member at the six person detachment.

A lone member greeted me at the detachment.

"Your trunk is here from Depot," he said warmly. "Want to go on patrol?"

Graduating Mounties have the majority of their issued work gear shipped ahead of them to their detachment. I found everything I needed just as I had packed it about a week before, so I changed into my uniform and off we went.

No sooner had we started our patrol when we received a call of a snowmobile accident. With lights and sirens blazing we headed to the scene. The single vehicle accident happened to be next to the local justice of the peace's residence. I got to meet the guy who would be approving my warrants and presiding over my bail hearings as well as other detachment members who had shown up to help. I met my trainer, the local paramedic and my sergeant, Larry Stright. My concerns about being accepted by the all-male team soon dissolved as I was warmly welcomed by all. This auspicious first shift certainly set the tone for what would be my next six years at Falcon Lake. Each member took me under their wing, provided mentorship and allowed ample freedom to grow and develop my skills as a peace officer.

But being the only female at the detachment was not always easy. Back in those days, it was a requirement for on-duty Mounties to wear headdress when outside or when performing certain duties like conducting "walk throughs" of bars. My early issue winter headdress was a special issue fur cap for women, and it was terribly ugly. At Depot, each of my troop mates and I gave our hats a pet name since they so closely resembled a live animal. The only redeeming quality to my hat was that it was warm in the minus-50 wintery environment in which I patrolled. My hat was different than that issued to my male counterparts in that it was cone shaped and featured pull-down flaps and ties. Although the women's RCMP fur cap was made of the same muskrat pelt and wool as the one for men, the male version featured no pull-down flaps and was in a decidedly more attractive shape. Bar patrons used to call me "cone head." We were also issued with a summer headdress which was different from the one for males. Sometimes during summer traffic stops, male motorists would eye my special female member issue pillbox-style forage cap and ask if I was a really a cop.

Of course, the easy solution was simply not to wear my hat. Even though policy strictly dictated that a headdress must be worn, I showed my rebellious streak and went hatless whenever possible. But one day, my sergeant pulled me aside outside the detachment for a chat. Larry had noticed I had been going about town with no hat and wanted to know what was up. I relayed to him my experiences with the female issue kit and asked him if he would be willing to wear my hat under such circumstances. Without another word, Larry went back into his residence, which was alongside the detachment, and emerged a few minutes later with his own male-issue forage cap and winter hat. He insisted that I take them as my own and wear them on duty as needed. My other colleagues never even questioned my new hat choice. And so began my days of wearing the male issue kit years before it was officially allowed.

After the hat incident, I realized how much my early positive experience was owed to the tone set by my forward thinking sergeant. Larry encouraged me to embrace policing without making me feel that my femininity took away from my ability to do a traditionally male job. Still, one of the early ideals I struggled with was that to be a Mountie, or a police officer in general, you had to be big and strong. My sergeant, who was five foot eight and only slightly taller than me, provided a concrete example of how this was a total misconception.

One day, Larry and I received a call that four park patrol officers were trapped in their van, which was being rocked by an irate mob of around thirty men. Larry and I pulled up to the scene. Surveying the angry crowd from the driver's seat, I wondered how on earth we could rescue the park patrol officers from such a large group of angry people. But my ever calm sergeant remained seated in the passenger seat of our police car as if he knew what would happen next.

After a few moments, the self-appointed leader of the group came over to give us his version of events. Apparently the angry mob was part of a campsite that felt the park patrol officers had been too gleeful in pouring out their liquor. Larry nodded sagely and listened understandingly as the irate leader vented his concerns. He was a pillar of empathy, even offering the leader a cigarette. Eventually, the leader's tone diminished and he began to match Larry's calm demeanour. The two became fast friends. Larry offered his opinion that the best thing to do would be for the mob to pack it in and for everyone to head back to their campsites for the night. To my amazement, the leader agreed and ordered the crowd to "shut it down." My sergeant taught me a valuable lesson that evening: It was possible to keep the peace without resorting to physical force.

Based on Larry's example, I focused on developing my own communication and negotiation skills. Soon after this incident, I was put to the test when I responded to a similar call about a noisy party at the beach. Patrolling alone, I arrived to find over 30 people enjoying a beach party in full swing. Undaunted, I took the same approach I had previously observed my sergeant take at the campsite. Sure enough, I was able to negotiate a peaceful end to the party with a self-appointed leader. I decided that my sergeant was a genius.

After thirty-three years in the RCMP, I can honestly say that my earlier experiences at Falcon Lake Detachment contributed significantly to my development as a police officer. I received a lot of support and mentorship from my sergeant, my trainer and the other senior officers posted with me during those early years. Their support paired with some diverse and crazy calls for service resulted in my life taking an enriching turn towards the person I am today.

After a while, I found the locals stopped calling me "cone head" and started calling me "bush woman." This was an honoured title bestowed by locals only upon a capable survivalist. I cherished this title along with every minute of my nowhere near ordinary career. I take my modern gender-neutral forage cap off to my first detachment at Falcon Lake. The small rural Manitoba detachment helped this city girl become a proud bush woman and will never be forgotten.

I'M POSTED WHERE?!
Sergeant Rhonda Leigh

In the spring of 1987, at the age of twenty-two, I completed my training as a member of the all-female Troop 14 at RCMP Depot Division in Regina, Saskatchewan. My fellow troop mates and I anxiously awaited the news of our first postings. Like my dad, retired Staff Sergeant Walt Leigh and my uncle, retired Corporal Bill Spencer, I'd signed on the dotted line, agreeing to go anywhere in Canada. It was an exciting time. We would soon be putting our training into action somewhere in the country, within a new community we would learn to call home. We all wondered where we would end up. Would some of us be posted close to one another? With whom would we be working? My old life as a university student seemed so far away as I prepared to begin this new career and life. My adventure was about to begin.

"I'm posted . . . where?"

I frantically surveyed a map of British Columbia. Vanderhoof. It was a tiny speck in the northern interior region of the province. I had never even heard of the town. I did some research and discovered that the small community boasted a population of approximately 6,500 people when you included a very large rural area between Prince George, Fraser Lake and Fort Saint James. I'd heard that towns including the words fort or lake in their names were remote and therefore a challenge to police. Well, according to the map, Vanderhoof was neither fort nor lake, but it was certainly surrounded by towns that were.

As we neared graduation, I called my new detachment a couple times to say hello and speak with my field trainer. When I finally managed to get through one Friday night, everyone was too busy to talk. Someone (perhaps my future trainer) shouted over the phone from the noisy cell block.

"Call back later!"

In the background, I could hear yelling. I knew I was in for an exciting experience at my new detachment.

A few weeks later, my troop and I graduated. There were mixed emotions as new close friends said their goodbyes, promised to keep in touch and prepared to disperse to locations across the country. Most of us ended up in British Columbia, and a few of us with postings relatively close geographically decided to travel out west together in a caravan. I purchased a fiery red Chrysler Daytona right out of the showroom from a dealership in Regina. Dad told me he thought it was too "stand-outish" and suggested I should try to blend in and not make such a statement at my new detachment. I, however, thought it matched nicely with my new red serge.

My fiery red Chrysler Daytona and I joined the caravan of troop mates traveling west. We crossed through Saskatchewan, then Alberta and finally into British Columbia. There, beneath a larger-than-life wooden statue of a logger, I said goodbye to a troop mate headed to Quesnel. We hugged, promising to call one another once settled. We were close enough geographically that we would be able to visit each other periodically. But for now, two close friends parted ways, starting their separate journeys to their respective detachments.

An hour later, I travelled down a steep hill on Highway 16.

As Vanderhoof came slowly into view, I found myself wondering, *Where is the actual town?*

I'd arrived. Vanderhoof had one Co-op store, one small movie theatre and only one traffic light down by the railroad tracks. I knew I was in for a very different experience than my hometown of Bedford, Nova Scotia.

I drove around the town at random until I found the detachment. Then, gathering up my courage, I went inside to meet the other members. I spoke with a constable at the front desk who furrowed his brow in confusion and shouted back into the office area to ask if anyone was expecting a recruit.

Oh no! I thought. *I'm at the wrong place!*

I'd traveled so far and long. I was exhausted but fought to hold back the tears of anxiety I was feeling. The constable saw my face and decided not to continue the joke. Instead, he laughed and welcomed me to Vanderhoof. The first regular female member ever posted there.

There were approximately a dozen regular members at Vanderhoof Detachment whose work was complemented by a small Highway Patrol Unit, several municipal employees, a public service employee, an Aboriginal special constable and a number of long-time auxiliary constable volunteers. It was a good detachment. We all learned how to work together and support one another. Of course there were challenging moments through the years as personalities differed, but we had a strong glue that connected us.

I lived in the basement suite of a home owned by a fabulous older couple who took me in as their own daughter. They were a huge part of my life. They were there for me when I felt lonely or when things got rough. Bud used to tease me, saying that if I kept washing my car so much, I'd wash the red right out. One day I offered to mow the lawn. The mower kicked up a stone that sailed through the air and smashed the windshield of Bud's truck. He laughed about it, though he never let me touch that mower again.

Vanderhoof was a very busy lumber town. The residents worked hard and they played hard. I quickly learned what it meant to be a police officer in a "working town." Not only that, but I learned how to survive as a female officer. Because I stood out in the crowd, I couldn't get away with any mistakes. Still, many of the town residents were quite accepting and in fact shared a sense of camaraderie with their local police, including me. Even the local radio personality and the newspaper editor were quite pro-police. They both had a sense of humour though, which sometimes made for some interesting publicity for the RCMP.

Late one afternoon, a jackrabbit ran in front of my police car. I tried to swerve and miss it, but was unsuccessful. I pulled over to the side of the road, picked up the deceased rabbit and gently laid it onto the grassy shoulder. I was a city girl and a bit upset about the whole thing and so I told one of my partners about what had happened. Of course, he thought my reaction was pretty funny and quickly shared the story with our local radio personality who, in turn, decided that the incident warranted a live, in-depth discussion on his show. The segment was called *No Easter Bunny This Year, Kids!*

And then there was Christmas 1988, when two colleagues and I were dispatched to an early morning domestic dispute at an apartment building. When we arrived, we saw a male dragging a female down the hallway. We yelled at him, identifying ourselves as police. His response was to pull out a gun and start shooting. We shouted for the residents who had poked their heads out of their doors to clear the narrow hallway. The suspect fired six shots but we still managed to tackle and handcuff him. As I stood up, I told my corporal that my shoulder felt warm. We found a small tear in the shoulder flash of my patrol jacket.

I hadn't been planning on telling my parents that I'd been shot, but my corporal insisted and it's a good thing he did because it hit newspapers across the country the very next day.

Woman RCMP officer shot! proclaimed one.

Female officer wounded in domestic dispute, read another.

A few of the local youth nicknamed me Constable "Ricochet" Rhonda. The name stuck and word of my new handle made it around town including to the newspaper editor. Of course, out of respect he didn't publish anything about it on that occasion, but he did remember it.

A while later, another corporal and I were called to a location far south of town where a logger had been killed by a falling tree. I rode in the passenger seat as my corporal drove our police truck along a snow-covered gravel road overlooking a steep embankment. Suddenly, we hit a snow drift! The truck skidded and then flipped onto the driver's side, sliding along that narrow roadway for what seemed like an eternity. I prayed that it wasn't yet my time; that we wouldn't tumble down that embankment. Finally, the truck slid to a stop. I found myself suspended by my seatbelt and my corporal had to push me up so that I could reach the passenger side window, roll it down and crawl out. I radioed for assistance, thankful that we had both been able to walk away from the accident relatively unscathed.

Once again, I was in the local newspaper, but this time I had company. *The Omineca Express* published a picture of a new and shiny-looking police truck along with a poem dedicated to Corporal "Flip" Anderson and Constable "Ricochet" Rhonda. I wasn't the only one with a nickname now.

In with the new, out with the old.
This one replaces the one that you rolled.
We'd like to remind you, as responsible cops,
that the wheels go on bottom, and the lights go on top!

– From Your Fans

We had definitely made an impression on the local news media. And it wasn't just them. Feelings of goodwill carried on to some of our interactions with the community as well. Vanderhoof was a small town where people worked together and, for the most part, looked out for one another. Some even looked out for their police officers on occasion.

One day I got a flat tire while out on Highway 16. As I dug around in the trunk for the tire iron, a vehicle pulled up behind me. Out piled a couple of fellows who offered their assistance. I was very much capable of changing my own tire, but they were sincere so I obliged them. I was thankful for the help, even more-so when they sped up the process so I could respond to a call.

Another time, I got called out to the highway to put down a moose that had been hit by a truck. I put on a brave and tough face as I took aim with my rifle. This was the first time I'd had to shoot an animal. I was startled when someone suddenly pulled me backwards. I then received a well-intentioned and much deserved lecture from an old-timer about standing so close to a moose in distress. I could've been killed by one kick from those massive hooves.

In Vanderhoof, we very often worked alone. A few times in my first year I called my dad up for some late night advice.

"Dad, I'm the 'Officer in Charge' of Vanderhoof Detachment!" I'd say.

I pictured him shaking his head as he laughed. I was always thankful for his late-night advice.

Many times I'd attend to reports of impaired drivers alone out on the highway in the middle of nowhere with backup a great distance away. Quite often the members of the public who had called in the report (usually long haul truckers) would sit in their vehicles, watch and wait until it was clear I had the situation under control with the suspect in my police vehicle before they left the scene.

For the most part, in Vanderhoof, if folks were not directly related, they were either friends, acquaintances or knew someone in common. This included the police. It meant that on Christmas, when the duties of my job prevented me from going home, I was never really alone. During the holidays, there were activities and events for both young and old. Decorations and lights lined the snow-covered streets. A sleigh pulled by majestic Clydesdales in jingling harnesses transported laughing children through the wintery wonderland. At the town Co-op store, a huge Christmas tree stood decorated by the town folk. We would sing carols and drink hot chocolate. Neighbours reconnected and friendships were renewed. It was a magical time.

Of course, there were many challenges to living and working in Vanderhoof. As a working town, Vanderhoof could be very busy. I was exposed to a variety of hair-raising calls that allowed me to develop into a skilled operational police officer. In my time there, I investigated assaults, home invasions, robberies and domestics. I comforted and held dying children and adults at traffic accidents before driving to their homes to tell their family members that their loved ones were gone. At times, I knew either those involved or their families. Such is the nature of policing in a small town.

In Vanderhoof, the police were not just the police. We were the SPCA, the fire department and the by-law officer. We were social workers, teachers and medical assistants. Even so, not everyone in town liked us. I was spat on and bled on. People threatened me with words. Sometimes they threatened me with weapons. I had my fair share of life-threatening calls but early in my career I developed trust in my own capabilities which served me well.

There was not much for teens to do in Vanderhoof. Shopping was limited, and the local movie theatre only played one movie, a month at a time. Often, youth would find their own fun and that sometimes meant trouble. But that is where I found my opportunity to give back to the community.

One day, the nearby Prince George Drug Section sent out a request looking for a lead volunteer for a new community-based project. I took it on, reaching out to all those community businesses, media folks and community members who'd built positive relationships with the police over the past several years. Together, we formed the Vanderhoof Drug and Alcohol Task Force. Our simple goal was to address addiction issues in our community and engage youth through planned community events.

We set up a meeting where adults and youth met to discuss what was important to them. I found that Vanderhoof's kids were not much different than kids anywhere. They wanted to hang out with each other on weekends. They wanted a skateboard park. Well, a skateboard park would take some time, but in the meantime we started by setting up regularly scheduled sports games where kids could play hockey or basketball against each other or even with off-duty police officers. We even had a games night one Friday at a local hall with food, organized games and a lots of volunteers. The town spoke of it for months. The Task Force won the BC Governor General's Award for service to the community which was a great affirmation that good things can be done when a community comes together.

My detachment was also responsible for providing policing services to the local Stoney Creek Indian Reserve and I made friends with a number of folks there. A son of one of the Band elders and his friends used to take me out horseback riding. The first time, I had to prove I could ride without a saddle. Things were going well until the horse spooked and I went for a tumble. But I brushed myself off and jumped back on to prove I wasn't hurt. Maybe I couldn't ride well without a saddle, but I was at least stubborn enough to get back on. It was good enough for them and I had the opportunity to ride many times after that. I even rode with real cowboys. Their boots were well-worn and dusty and their shirts were stained with sweat. These weren't city boys who wear new hats and boots pristine from the store in an attempt to look the part of cowboy. These were real working guys. Even though I was an outsider to the community and would eventually transfer to a different posting in the RCMP, I made a point of making this connection. They had graciously let me ride their horses and I wanted to help out with some of their work as a way to say thank you.

One day while I accompanied the guys on a roundup, I saw a lone cow standing apart from the group at the other end of the meadow. Thinking I was smart, I headed over to get it to regroup with the others. But as we cantered over, my horse began getting a little skittish. Not knowing why, I urged her on until I saw a real cowboy cantering towards me. On his face he wore an expression of mirth mixed with concern. Once he reached me, he quickly pointed out that I should stop bothering the bull! City girl... I quickly returned to the group of cows where I took the good-natured teasing from the other cowboys there with a smile.

I enjoyed spending time on the reserve, both on and off duty. I'd chat with the kids and learn a little of their heritage and culture from the elders. I had the opportunity to attend events at the potlatch building where I enjoyed watching the dancers, dressed in their beautiful, vibrant, hand-made costume. I learned about natural medicines derived from local plants and watched their expert craftswomen sew and bead moccasins. A respected female elder even honoured me by making me my own beautiful pair.

The well-respected elder was very wise, proud and kind. I used to love popping by her log home near Nulki Lake to enjoy a cup of tea along with dried salmon, bannock and homemade jam. She kept a smoke hut in the yard and the delicious smell of fish and smoke were ever-present. When I'd reach for seconds of bannock, she'd smile and remind me that it was cooked in fat. But it was such a treat! I'd return the smile and say I didn't care, promising myself to add an extra mile to my run that evening.

The elder and her family had a special relationship with the Vanderhoof RCMP that went back to a tragic incident that had happened years before. At that time, police had rendered assistance, and as a thank you, each year since then, the RCMP had been honoured with a day at the family fishing camp. Together, we would walk a trail through the woods down to the water where a wonderful dinner of smoked salmon with all the trimmings awaited us. I looked forward to the yearly trek as I always learned something new and gained a better understanding of the people I served.

Our family recently lost my uncle Corporal Bill Spencer after his brief battle with cancer. He'd joined the RCMP in 1972 and retired after thirty-six years serving in several small communities in Northern Manitoba including Flin Flon and The Pas. Both he and my father knew how important it was to integrate into the communities they served. I'm so thankful for their example. In particular, my dad passed RCMP values on to me through his stories, words of wisdom and encouragement. These lessons I have applied again and again over the past twenty-nine years of my career, starting with Vanderhoof.

The memories I've made have been shared over the years during coffee breaks in many detachments. My hope is that new members will also choose to immerse themselves in their local communities. I hope that they too will make lifelong friends with their coworkers and the neighbours alongside whom they raise their families, that they will benefit from freely volunteering their time at community events, and that they will experience professional and personal growth from giving back.

Just like I did in Vanderhoof, that little speck on the map.

The author dedicates her story to her dad, Staff Sergeant Walt Leigh (Ret.) and her late uncle, Corporal Bill Spencer (Ret.).

#GDIVTRAVELS: A CIVILIAN MEMBER EXPLORES
THE NORTHWEST TERRITORIES
Jean C. Turner, Civilian Member

I landed at the small Yellowknife Airport eager to start my Arctic adventure. As a civilian member of the RCMP, or "CM" as we are often called, I employ specialized skills to support front-line policing. I specialize in communications and work in Ontario's Corporate Communications and Media Relations Unit. Generally, my job keeps me close to home. But the winter of 2012 was a different matter. I'd been invited to participate in a National Communications Services exchange program and had travelled to the Northwest Territories (designated as "G Division" by the RCMP) to learn about the division's best practices in communication.

I've worked all my life in the same city I grew up in, and my annual travel has largely been limited to visiting resort destinations in the winter. One time, I took a road trip to New Brunswick and Prince Edward Island. You can therefore imagine how ecstatic I was when I stepped off that plane. I was eager to meet the locals, talk with some of the police officers and of course see the aurora borealis, and maybe a polar bear or two.

I was greeted at the gate by my smiling host. Sergeant Wes Heron proved to be a wealth of knowledge.

"This airport might look small, but it handles close to 70,000 inbound and outbound aircraft movements a year," he said knowledgeably. "There's an average of 55 flights departing every single day."

I could see he had a strong sense of pride for the community he policed.

On the way out to the parking lot, Wes added that the G Division RCMP maintained a hangar for its air section just south of the regular terminal used by the general public. This was my first clue that air travel was a big deal in the Northwest Territories. Over the next few days, this would become even clearer.

That evening I settled into my hotel room. Being the social media enthusiast that I am, I had decided to tweet my Arctic Adventure using the hashtag #gdivtravels. Many coworkers and friends were following #gdivtravels, eager to see my pictures and experience the north along with me. But arriving in Yellowknife, I'd quickly learned that Internet access is not a guarantee up north. The harsh environments and rural locations that make the region so unique also mean that much of the infrastructure needed to support access is lacking. My vision of my as-they-happened tweets going viral quickly faded after touching down in Yellowknife. But with internet access at my hotel, I knew I'd be able to log in each evening, send out a few photographs and recap my day. This would be a different approach to technology and social media than I was used to. Back home in the city, I had instant internet access at my fingertips 24 hours a day. Life up north was definitely different.

The next morning, I visited the G Division RCMP Operational Communications Centre (OCC) which was located near the Yellowknife Airport. Here, dispatchers coordinate police operations across the entire division. The people who work here are the lifeline for police officers working alone in various northern communities. They are the heart and soul of the division.

I chatted with some of the people working that morning. The atmosphere was reasonably relaxed as we talked about their families, their jobs and life up north. The realities of supporting police efforts in the north make an already challenging job even more so. G Division OCC operators are responsible for dispatching police services across an expansive 1,171,918 square kilometre land mass. There are 11 official languages with at least twice as many dialects, and in the remote territory, many residences don't have an actual address. It is often difficult to identify exactly where to send police services. But despite these challenges, I heard many stories about how happy these people were to live and work up north. It can be a unique experience, unlike any other.

Suddenly, the mood in the OCC shifted. One of the dispatchers had received a plane in distress call. In a flurry of activity, the dispatchers coordinated the response. Police officers were dispatched to set up roadblocks and other emergency responders were put on ready status. Everyone prepared for the worst.

Looking out the window of the OCC, I could see a Buffalo Air cargo plane circling the landing strip. The landing gear wouldn't engage. In the communications centre, the atmosphere was tense. Dispatchers provided direction over the radio. Fingers flew over keyboards. Eyes remained fixed on screens.

The pilot advised he was going to perform a touch-and-go maneuver in an attempt to release a stuck landing gear. I watched as the large plane came in as if for a landing and then bounced off the tarmac. The pilot was unsuccessful in knocking the landing gear loose. He soared overhead and circled, making a second attempt which was also unsuccessful. After the third attempt failed, the decision was made to make an emergency landing on just one wheel!

The plane came in for a landing and touched down, laying down sparks as it slid along the tarmac. The entire OCC seemed to hold its collective breath. The plane slid along for what seemed like an eternity before finally screeching to a halt. There was silence on the radio. And finally, an update: the plane was down and all five persons aboard were safe. I couldn't believe it. It was like being in a live episode of *Ice Pilots*. This experience was later capped off with a personal tour of the Buffalo Air hangar by none other than Mikey McBryan himself (star of television's *Ice Pilots*). I got to see the damage to the plane. It looked serious, but Mikey was confident it could be fixed.

As an ice pilot, Mikey and others like him, provide a key service to the Arctic community. Air services are the lifeline to many communities in the Northwest Territories and are relied on extensively to transport everything from food and clothing to household furniture and hunting equipment. The RCMP are no exception when it comes to relying heavily on air support. For a G Division member, responding to a call often requires hopping on a plane to get to a remote or isolated location. Of course, the element of surprise is gone as soon as the entire settlement sees you coming in a plane. For this reason, northern police officers develop strong communication and negotiation skills.

Of course, it's not always urgent calls for service or emergency situations that keep the RCMP Air Services operating day in and out. While I was visiting, Yellowknife members were dispatched on a routine transport of several prisoners from Inuvik to the capital city for court. When they invited me to go along with them, I jumped at the chance.

Inuvik is located two degrees above the Arctic Circle on the scenic Mackenzie River. The traditional homeland of the Inuvialuit and Gwich'in peoples, today it is home to approximately 3,500 residents and an RCMP detachment consisting of sixteen regular members.

The two and a half hour flight from Yellowknife to Inuvik was amazing. I had an unobstructed bird's eye view of the minus twenty-seven degree Celsius winter landscape and rugged terrain. As harsh as the environment was, it looked beautiful to me, soaring far above. I sat in wide-eyed wonder as Wes, who had accompanied me on the flight, pointed out scattered Inuit communities and ice roads that had been carved into vast frozen lakes. I eagerly anticipated our arrival. I was excited to set foot inside the Arctic Circle for the first time.

When we landed we were met by the gregarious detachment commander Staff Sergeant Wayne Norris who drove us to Inuvik Detachment. We travelled on some of the very same ice roads I'd seen from above during our flight. As he expertly maneuvered his truck on the icy surface, Wayne told me about some of the unique dangers of traveling in the Arctic. As he explained, when two vehicles pass on an ice road, the drivers slow down because the opposing waves of force created by two vehicles passing rapidly can cause waves far below the surface which can crack the ice. Yet another thing police officers down south don't have to worry about.

The town looked quite different from the city where I live. The presence of permafrost means that buildings have to be built on piles or stilts. As we travelled through town, Wes told me about the above ground sheds called utilidors that heated water and the accompanying above ground lines called utilidettes that carried water in and sewage out of the brightly coloured row houses that have become somewhat of a trademark of the town.

But despite the obvious differences in urban landscape, I noticed some similarities to my life in the big city. As it turned out, Inuvik, like much of Canada's North, is quite ethnically diverse. I never expected to see a mosque north of the 60th parallel and I was pleasantly surprised to meet many people of various backgrounds. As I learned, aside from the obvious tourism element, many "southerners" (both Mountie and civilian) travel to Canada's north for work and, after falling in love with the region, never leave. I found that the cliché of northern police work being only for men was just that, a cliché. I met a number of female police officers, some specialists in their fields, who told me that they absolutely loved life in the North.

On the flight back to Yellowknife, the pilot let me sit up front with him in the cockpit. Unlike the ice plane incident from earlier that morning, our flight ended uneventfully. Of course this is really what you hope for with a plane full of prisoners.

On my last night in Yellowknife, I was determined to see the amazing celestial phenomenon known as the aurora borealis. This meant I had to stay up well past midnight. Dressed warmly in northern attire including long johns, a feather-filled parka, beaver mittens, and a toque, I spent my last few hours in the Northwest Territories standing outside my hotel, camera in hand, gazing skyward.

I wasn't disappointed. Waves of coloured lights danced across the sky. As I watched, mesmerized by the magic of the aurora borealis, I thought about how this trip had given me a much deeper respect for our RCMP police officers and dispatchers working up north. I also thought about my role as a communications specialist. The goal of our policing operations Canada-wide is successful investigation, catching the "bad guy" and keeping Canadians safe. I'd always seen my role as facilitating and communicating operational successes as well as encouraging and empowering people to play a role in the safety and security of their own communities. #gdivtravels showed me the great potential that social media can play in sharing the stories of the RCMP. My trip up north showed me the diversity of experiences in the Force and the unique challenges of sharing them with limited access.

There are so many more things that I could tell you about my trip up north, but I will save the stories of buffalo meat, old gold mines and dog mushing for another time. G Division was a whirlwind of new sights, sounds and life experiences that I will never forget. All of the people I met were amazing, hearty folks, rich both in stories and in life

Whenever I see a Canada Goose parka, I will think of G Division. Whenever the snow squeaks beneath my boots (because you haven't heard snow squeak until you have been to the Arctic Circle) I will think of G Division. And although I never did get to see a polar bear, the Northwest Territories has given me a love and affection for our Canadian north and its people that I will carry with me always.

It is no secret. I tell anyone who asks (and some who do not) that I love my job and I am a proud civilian member of the Royal Canadian Mounted Police. And now you have just a little taste of why.

IT'S 2014! WHAT DO YOU MEAN I'M THE ONLY FEMALE?
Constable Jennifer Dowden

Cubical life was getting to me. I wanted to do something different, something new. I'd enjoyed my three month secondment to International Operations and Policing Development in Ottawa, assisting with the coordination and monitoring of peace operation deployments to Latin America and the Caribbean. It was a rare position that few constables have the opportunity to hold and they'd offered to extend my time there, but I missed being on the go and needed a change. I craved the unique challenges and adventures attainable in the field. I needed to get back into the operational scene.

My director suggested that I might enjoy working in the Shiprider Unit. He had previously worked on the project which was still relatively new. Members of the Shiprider program are specially trained peace officers designated to enforce the law on both sides of the United States-Canadian border. The program is all about partnership and teamwork. RCMP Shiprider members work together with members of the program from the United States Coast Guard to patrol waterways between the two countries. At the time, there were only two teams: one in Windsor, Ontario and one in Vancouver, British Columbia. But there were plans to expand the program to the Niagara Falls region as well as the Kingston area. After a conversation with my director, I became excited to apply. I never hesitate when an opportunity presents itself.

I sent my application in and it was accepted but this did not mean that the job was mine. I still had to pass the Shiprider course. I received the nod to attend the ten day course in Charleston, South Carolina and began preparing myself as best I could.

I suppose some people would assume I am a natural mariner, being from Newfoundland and all, but nothing could be further from the truth. Sure, I have managed to get out on a few whale watching tours over the years, but skillfully operating a law enforcement vessel is absolutely nothing like playing tourist on a pleasure cruise. I studied the pre-course materials and followed up with the RCMP coordinator overseeing the course from Ottawa on a regular basis to ensure that I was doing everything humanly possible to pass the course, but, more importantly, prevent myself from embarrassment. It was during one of these conversations that I was informed that I was the only female on the course.

"The *only* female?" I asked. "It's 2014. What do you mean I'm the *only* female?"

There were seven RCMP officers including me traveling to Charleston. Our course was administered by the United States Coast Guard and we would be learning alongside twenty-one members of their organization. Not only was I the only female Mountie attending the course, I was the only female student in the entire group—twenty-seven men and me. Now I had even more of a reason to prove that I was up for the challenge.

In preparation for the course, the organizers from the RCMP along with a liaison officer from the United States Coast Guard, held a conference call with all seven RCMP candidates on the line. The other candidates called in from all over Canada; I knew none of them. On the call I ensured my voice was even in tone and kept my answers short, to the point and professional. At least they would think I *sounded* cut out for the job. Things seemed to be going well and I started to think I might fit in, but then one of the coordinators mentioned to the group that I was the only candidate who had completed the required homework prior to the course commencement.

Really!?

It was already clear that I was the only female going on the course; now I sounded like the always unpopular keener of the group. This was the last thing I wanted. So much for flying under the radar.

Near the end of the conference call, one last wrench was thrown into the gears of my plan to blend in with the boys: The announcement of a swim class. At first I thought it was a joke. It was not a joke. We received a friendly reminder not to wear a two-piece swimsuit as some pool activities would not be conducive to such attire. It could have been a way to poke fun at the males in the group, but I jumped on the opportunity to get a laugh and spoke up, assuring everyone that I had no intention of donning a two-piece. I'm not the sensitive type and can laugh at my own expense. Now they knew that too.

The day finally arrived and I flew to South Carolina. I specifically chose to dress professionally. I carried myself with confidence and walked with a purpose. I was "all business." Outside the Charleston International Airport I found a bus driver standing on the curb, holding a sign that read *Federal Law Enforcement Training Centre*. He pointed to an old white school bus further down in the parking area and told me to wait onboard. I began the hike down the road solo, as he stayed to wait for the other arrivals.

The bus was old and there was no storage underneath so I had to wedge my heavy suitcase through the narrow passenger entrance and up three high steps. Forgetting all graces, I cursed and swore as I heaved my suitcase to chest level, jammed it up the steep, narrow stairs and set it down unceremoniously on the upper level. Only when I stood up, unencumbered from my burden, did I see the dozen pairs of eyes staring at me. They were all young men, each sporting a closely shaved head. These were likely some of my American classmates. They all sat there, silently staring at me. I ignored the urge to abandon my suitcase and walk right off that bus.

Instead, I straightened my blazer and wiping hair out of my face, casually stated, "Oh, the bus isn't empty."

And with that, I carried on, stowed my suitcase and found a seat. At least I *sounded* like a sailor. Intimidating, right?

On the first day of the course we were assigned seating. I found my place amongst three United States Coast Guards at the front of the classroom. After formal introductions from the instructors, the candidate introductions began. I had to sound like I was supposed to be there. Smart. Strong. Qualified. Sea worthy! The others talked about their years of service with the Coast Guard and the type of marine-related work they had done. They were all young, *real* young. They all had lots of boating experience. And then it was my turn. My heart was racing. I had this all thought out. I was ready to impress.

"I'm Constable Jennifer Dowden of the Royal Canadian Mounted Police. I am the token female on this course and I'm a 'Newfie' to boot."

With a smile, I received the comforting, supportive laughter from the class. I assumed the Americans knew what a "Newfie" was. The ice was broken and I think everyone needed it. After that, I proceeded to share my experience in the Force. I admitted my lack of boating experience but expressed my enthusiasm to learn. I think they all appreciated my honesty and straightforwardness.

On the second day of the course, I came back from lunch to find that someone had posted a poster-sized copy of one of my old Musical Ride trading cards at the front of the room. I had served on the Musical Ride a few years earlier. Each year, every member of the Ride has a special trading card made featuring a picture of them with their horse with some basic tombstone data on the back. The cards are given out at Musical Ride performances, usually to kids. I wondered who had managed to snag one of mine and gone through the effort to display it for the class to see. It featured me in red serge, with my horse Dancer from our 2012 tour. Everyone seemed to be waiting for my reaction. I smiled and quietly sat down.

"Is that *you*?" asked one of my classmates from the United States Coast Guard.

It seemed the "Coasties" were impressed. A real Mountie in a red jacket with a *horse*! I was like a legend to them, and I can't lie: Instead of feeling embarrassment, I felt proud.

"Yeah, I was on the ride for four years," I told them.

There was a lot of attention directed my way, but for a positive reason. So many curious questions … and suddenly, I fit in. I was one of the boys. No I wasn't. I was *the girl*.

It was inevitable: swim class. Of course, this part was voluntary for everyone; I didn't have to do it. But I was ready to drown in that pool if it meant proving to the boys that I deserved to be there. I quickly changed in the washroom and walked out the door to the pool before I could change my mind. I just wanted it to be over.

When I walked out on that pool deck that day, I felt the looks. They were the "I'm not looking, but I'm looking" looks from the inquisitive, stealthily wandering eyes. Thankfully, this was short lived. We had work to do.

I swallowed more water that day than I care to remember and my teeth remain stark white from all that chlorine. My lungs burned and my legs ached. My classmates and I treaded water in the deepest part of the pool holding bricks over our heads. We sank to the bottom of the pool wearing our duty belts with added weight. I raced some of the guys in the swim, and volunteered to be first in line to climb the Jacob's Ladder to the ceiling. I climbed steadily to the top of the flimsy rope ladder, feeling every muscle in my tired arms and legs. When I reached the top, I had to step off the ladder, aiming my legs straight down towards the pool. My hands were burning on the rope. I was holding my entire body weight. Waiting. When I was given the "okay" from an instructor below, I released the rope and plunged into the pool feet first, straight as a whip. When I emerged from the bottom of the pool, I heard applause and cheers from my classmates—no, my *teammates*. We cheered for each and every person after they completed their jump.

As the course went on, I was no longer the "token female" I'd labeled myself on day one. By graduation, I was a colleague who had successfully completed the course with support and encouragement from my peers. The same support and encouragement I showed to each of them. I shook hands with my new partners who looked forward to working with me on the water. There was a mutual respect. I had taught others how to treat me by the way I interacted with them. I could laugh at myself, stand up for myself, blend in and stand out, all at the same time. This was a lesson I enjoyed learning. I cannot wait for the next opportunity.

MY FIRST POSTING
Corporal Louise Savard

My first transfer in the RCMP had been approved. In a few short months, I would be leaving my first posting at Florenceville, New Brunswick for new adventures elsewhere at another detachment. Standing before my stern sergeant, I never thought that I would ever be in his office to receive a compliment. I had only been at the posting for a few years, but in that time, this small, brand new, woman Mountie had somehow earned the respect of her supervisor and coworkers. Considering that this all happened in the 1980s, I considered it a triumph.

During the years that we worked together, my sergeant and I learned to respect each other and I learned a lot from him. Now, in his office he told me that he was sad I was leaving the detachment, that I was a good member and that my shoes would be hard to fill. Coming from him, this was a great compliment and confirmed not only that I'd proven myself to be a competent cop, but that I belonged. Our first introduction had gone quite differently.

I will never forget the period in November 1986. I just graduated from Depot with an intended posting I had never heard of. When I could not locate Florenceville on a map of New Brunswick, I turned to the "Mountie grapevine" to get information. I asked fellow recruits from the province if they knew of my destination.

Someone told me, "It's between Edmunston and Fredericton. When you drive on the highway you can't blink or you'll miss it."

I was also told that Florenceville was called "McCain Country." The McCain family, who are well known for introducing the frozen French fry amongst other products dominated the area. Almost everyone in and around Florenceville worked for McCain Foods Limited which was based in town.

Naturally, I also asked some questions about the small town's seven man detachment where I would be working.

"Well the guy in charge there doesn't like women and doesn't like French," one person told me.

"I heard they call the boss 'Ayatollah' behind his back," said another. "He's a tough man."

Yikes, I thought. *What am I getting myself into?*

Here I was, a French Canadian woman from Montreal, posted to a tiny, all-male detachment in the middle of nowhere where I met all the criteria on the sergeant's list of things he hated. I realized that I was likely in for quite an interesting experience.

Undaunted, I phoned my detachment and spoke to my trainer. He seemed reasonable on the phone. He told me they'd located an apartment for me and gave me some details to facilitate my move. I was appreciative of his efforts, as rental housing in Florenceville was hard to find. So off I went to New Brunswick, taking the Trans-Canada Highway east from Regina. In New Brunswick, I drove past Edmunston. I was careful not to blink as I did not want to miss my new town.

Upon my arrival at Florenceville Detachment I was greeted by the public servant who turned out to be a real sweetheart. I also met my trainer. He was a rugged six foot something man with distinguished red hair. I would have loved to have known what he was thinking, peering down at me, the first female to be posted to the detachment, standing at just five feet tall.

I then met the detachment's Officer in Charge. The infamous sergeant.

"SAVARD!" he bellowed. "Can I see you in my office?" It wasn't really a request.

I was anxious and nervous about what he was going to say. He closed the door behind me when I entered his office. It was just him and I.

"You get paid the same salary as the men," he said. "So I expect you to do the same work as them."

"I don't expect to do any less. I'm here to work, Sir," I replied, using the honorific technically reserved for the rank of inspector and above.

He seemed satisfied with my answer.

"I just wanted to make sure we understood each other," he said.

There it was, out in the open. So here I was, ready to work. At the small detachment, I didn't have the luxury of a long training period and after a week or so, I found myself working the night shift on my own. I was given the keys to a police car and told to explore the area.

While on patrol, I went to the area known as Bath along the Saint John River. Driving on the main road, I encountered a vehicle travelling towards me in the opposite lane. As we neared each other, I noticed that the other vehicle was drifting in and out of its lane and swerving. I got on the radio to my dispatcher and advised her that I was about to go after an impaired driver. My dispatcher told me she would call backup from a neighbouring detachment.

I activated my police lights and siren for the first time in my career and went after the vehicle. I felt a rush of adrenaline as I closed the distance between the suspect vehicle and my police car. But before I could pull it over, the vehicle stopped in front of a house. A man got out of the driver's side and ran inside.

I updated my dispatcher, who reminded me to wait for the backup that was already on the way. I waited impatiently, eager to make my first arrest.

Soon, a woman exited the house and strode towards my police car.

"I want him out of my house," she said, firmly.

I asked her who "he" was.

"He's my ex-boyfriend," was the reply. "I'm going to work and I want him out before I come back."

I assured her he would be out. She left.

Not too long after, my backup arrived. My two partners and I entered the house to search for my suspect. My heart pumped rapidly in my chest. He was hiding from us. I employed the room clearing techniques I'd learned just a short time ago at Depot. My time in training in Regina felt like it was a whole world away.

Suddenly, I found him! He had been hiding behind a door. I affected my first arrest and took him in for impaired driving.

There were no pats on the back or fireworks. I was just doing my job. But that first arrest set the stage for many more opportunities to demonstrate my ability to get the job done. My sergeant grew to trust my skills. He knew that if he asked me to complete a task, I would do it well and in a timely manner. In the end, I learned that respect has little to do with size or gender and a lot to do with commitment and heart.

That day, as I said goodbye to my sergeant, I felt as if I stood six feet tall. I was proud to be a member of the RCMP.

THE GIFT OF INUUQATIGIITSIARNIQ[1]
Sergeant Yvonne H. Niego

My father was born in an igloo and lived nomadically off the Arctic tundra for the first decade of his life in an area known today as Nunavut. He lived as Inuit had lived for a few thousand years. He was strong, proud, resilient and adaptable. My father's family had a close bond to the RCMP. His uncle served as RCMP special constable, running the dog sleds and assisting regular members patrolling the far-flung communities of the north. The values of my father and the cultural grounding of our family set my feet on the path leading to a life in the RCMP.

I grew up in Baker Lake, Nunavut, the geographical centre of Canada and the only mainland Inuit community in the country. It was a changing era in the north. RCMP special constables were still hired from among our people, but no longer were there any sled dog patrols. Our communities had evolved too. The igloos of my father's generation began to disappear, replaced with permanent homes built of wood, glass and metal. Still, my father instilled in me the values of his generation. It was through his coffee time visits at the local Baker Lake RCMP Detachment with me, his first born, latched to his side, that I came to trust and admire the iconic Mountie. My father made it his duty to protect and maintain the relationship between the Inuit community and the RCMP. A large percentage of the local people couldn't speak English or French, and Mounties have an even harder time learning the local dialect of Inuktitut, the language of the Inuit in the eastern Arctic. My father knew that lack of communication would mean problems ahead, and so he would personally welcome each new police officer

---

[1] pronounced "ee-new-kha-tee-gheet'-see-arh-nikh"

to the tiny Baker Lake Detachment, laying the groundwork for a long-lasting mutual relationship of trust.

After growing up a bit, I went away to school "down south" in Calgary, Alberta. I was very likely the first homegrown Baker kid to make it to university. Coming home to Baker, I found some work to keep me busy as an RCMP summer student. This soon developed into a job as a matron in the cellblock, and eventually a spot in the RCMP Aboriginal Constable Development Program. Working for the Force came naturally. I'd inherited Dad's keen ability to moderate relationships, or what we call "keeping the peace." I eventually signed up to become a regular member.

Graduating from Depot, I became the first Inuk woman to complete the regular six month basic recruit training. I began my career in Iqaluit and eventually returned to Baker Lake where I worked for a number of years. My husband and I had three kids and I took a few years off for them. Coming back from leave, I was a new person. During my time off I had gained a lot of experience in managing people, granted, people half my size. But balancing family, my job and the rigours of working in the north was more challenging than I'd expected. In Nunavut and the Northwest Territories, virtually every posting requires that members are available twenty-four hours a day and seven days a week. If you aren't on shift, you're on call. Another challenge is that members in the Arctic must transfer to different posts every two or three years. Many postings are remote, isolated and located within fly-in communities. I had the added challenge of working in a community where almost everyone was related to me by either blood or marriage.

Finally, after several years of repeated transfers to remote postings, I mustered the courage to move our family south to Ottawa.

I had spent my entire life grounded in the values of humanity, social justice, and being connected responsibly to the land. In moving to the city my biggest difficulty was not the job, but learning the local etiquette. I knew nothing of growing or maintaining weedless grass. I'd had no idea how fast trees grew or how often they require trimming. I'd not considered, when purchasing our home, that each fall the enormous trees in our new front yard would dump millions of leaves requiring hours of raking. Learning and adopting practices in keeping with the local etiquette, I developed an incredible sense of respect for my fellow Mounties who'd journeyed to *my* homeland to work in an environment as foreign to them as grass and trees were to me.

While working in Ottawa, I had the opportunity to speak publicly on issues related to women in policing and missing and murdered Aboriginal women. On my first speaking engagement, I was to present to a few hundred people. I didn't feel that I was ready. During this time, it happened that I received very different kinds of support and edification from three people who are very important to me. First, I reached out to my beloved father, whom I saw as an elder to my people. We talked about relational challenges between men and women.

"The roles have changed," he said.

He was right. Gender roles had changed. The division between men and women was not as clear as it once had been. The old tradition of women taking charge of everything in the home while the men worked outside was not always the norm. This was definitely my experience as a part of the Inuit community and, I imagine, the experience of a lot of Canadian women in our time. Today, both men and women must find a balance between the jobs we work and the duties at home. We must learn to share and be "in sync."

On the morning of my presentation, I got ready at home, still feeling somewhat unprepared. I told my youngest that I had a big day of speaking to many people ahead.

My daughter looked at me and said, "Mom, you look pretty today."

She shot me a smile as I saw her off to the bus stop for school. She'd always had a keen sense of people and knew me well. She'd known just what I'd needed to hear.

I turned to my husband. "What am I to say? How can I do this?"

He gave me the answer I needed: "Just...don't...cry."

My husband has always known when I've needed to laugh. My family has never failed to be the source of support I need.

I eventually returned home with my family, this time as the first Nunavut Inuk woman promoted to the rank of corporal. It felt good to be home. Again, in keeping with the values taught by my father, my work became about people and their relationship with the land and each other. I developed my own cultural orientation for RCMP members and their families moving to Nunavut and focused on building trust with the community through communication both as the leader of Nunavut's Critical Incident Negotiation Team and as a media spokesperson for the Force.

I was recently honoured as a recipient of the International Association of Women Police Community Service Award. This proud moment was not just a first for an Inuk woman, but one for any member of the RCMP. As I prepared for my acceptance speech, I reflected on all my father and my years of experience in the RCMP had taught me: That if we can approach each other with an attitude of respect, listen and learn, and put in a few kind words or actions for someone in need, we will all be in a better place. In Inuktitut, we call it *Inuuqatigiitsiarniq*. It is the principle of caring for people, caring for relationships and embracing human rights.

THE HEAD TURNER
Corporal Donna Morse, née Burns (Ret.)

In March 1975, twenty-nine troop mates and I graduated from Depot, becoming the first women employed as regular members in the RCMP. We set off in every direction across Canada to commence our careers in various postings. I was sent to Port Alberni, British Columbia.

Since its inception in 1873, the RCMP had been strictly dominated by male officers. When I arrived at my first post, it signalled changing times. But sometimes people find change hard. Many people questioned whether a female would be able to carry out the duties of a serving police officer. Although a few Canadian municipal police forces did have a small number of women serving in active policing roles, this was the first time that the RCMP would have females wearing the uniform and patrolling the streets of both rural and urban centres. Of course there were questions. In fairness, who wouldn't have questions when such a significant transition had occurred that would forever change the fabric of our national police force?

I arrived at my new post a few days after graduation. I was ready to work and naïvely thought that my presence at the detachment was no big deal, that it wouldn't generate any curiosity amongst the citizens and the male officers living and working in the mid-sized lumber and fishing town.

Some people might be surprised to learn that I found myself feeling comfortable with many of my co-workers within days of settling in at my detachment. I quickly became friends with some of the male officers, their wives and other people within the community. Some members of the public, though, felt it was odd to see a female police officer around town. Quite often, people would stop their cars in the middle of the road to take a second look at me sitting in my police car. Sometimes pedestrians would pause in the middle of the crosswalk to stare and point at me, in some cases getting caught in the road when the light changed for oncoming traffic. Children would consistently stop and wave to me, laughing at the unusual sight of a female in uniform behind the wheel of a police cruiser.

I had heard that police in general sometimes drew attention. But quite soon after arriving in Port Alberni, I became fully aware that the finger pointing and staring was reserved especially for me. While I didn't much prefer this type of attention, what could I do but wave and smile back at them before continuing on my way? I think, though, that all this was quite disturbing to my trainer.

It soon became clear to me that male officers were preferred by both female and male complainants. When I attended a complaint with a male partner, witnesses would often want to talk to him instead of me. When this happened early on, I didn't make it a big issue. Instead, I listened and observed. I learned a lot from my partners this way and within a short period of time I had opportunities to attend calls on my own. Then I was only too happy to inform the complainant that I was an actual trained police officer and capable of handling whatever issue they had. Although this attitude was definitely more prevalent forty years ago, I did experience similar responses from citizens even up to when I retired in 1995. Over the course of my service, there were several occasions when I would ask a question and the witness would automatically direct their answer to my male partner whether he was junior to me in service or not. Sometimes complainants actually tried to refuse discussing their issue with a female member. I'm hopeful that these attitudes have changed in the 21st Century.

Of course, it was not all just harmless curiosity or general rudeness. Early in my time in Port Alberni, some of the "notorious" citizens in town felt that it would be fun to harass and follow me.

I imagine they were thinking, *what could a female police officer do?*

Many times, these individuals would park their vehicles on the street outside my apartment to "keep an eye" on me and follow me around town both while I was working and on days off. They eventually escalated to phoning in false complaints to the detachment in hopes that I would be the attending officer. This went on for a number of weeks. It was annoying and scary, but I refused to back down. I later had the pleasure of arresting them on a number of occasions. I was able to hold my own, but it was also nice to know that my male counterparts had my back. After a period of time, they made sure that the activity came to an end.

All in all, I had an incredible time in Port Alberni and, in the end, my colleagues all came through in helping me build a good foundation for my future policing career. The memories of the time I spent policing that little island municipality will stay with me always.

NO PRINCE CHARMING
Inspector Ruth Roy

When I joined the RCMP thirty-three years ago, I was posted to Canada's west coast. I was far away from my family, my home and my east coast. It was quite daunting being on my own at the age of nineteen and working in a profession that came with high expectations. I remember being lonely at first and worried that I would not be able to do the work. However, it was in the first six months on the job that I learned the most valuable lesson of my career: Police work is more about being able to deal with people than it is about being physically tough. How I treated others was often a reflection of how they reacted to me as a person and as a police officer.

My trainer was "old school," and did not believe that women should be police officers. He was a man who liked to strong-arm people—a rough and tumble, beat them down, ask questions later kind of guy. This was a different era in Canada. It was prior to the introduction of the *Canadian Charter of Rights and Freedoms*, so my trainer was not challenged about how he treated people.

Sometimes after choking out a suspect he would look at me and say, "Why didn't you do that?"

I was intimidated by my trainer, so while I often felt the level of force he'd applied had been uncalled for, I remained silent.

After three months of training I was finally permitted to work on my own. It was a nice reprieve to be able to patrol in my police car without having my trainer yelling at me. While out patrolling one morning early in my first summer, I met a man who would change my life. Not my "prince charming," but still someone who had a huge impact on who I became as a police officer and as a person.

The shift was just starting and the members of my watch were preparing for the day ahead. A call came in about a disturbance at the local gospel mission. The mission provided meals to homeless and street people, often those struggling with addiction. There was one key rule: if you wanted to hang out there, you had to be sober. As a result, mission staff would often call us to remove someone from the property who was intoxicated. On that particular morning, I responded to the call.

When I arrived at scene, I could hear raised voices coming from the eating area located in the rear of the mission. I headed over and saw the massive back of a male who was having words with the petite minister who managed the place. I overheard the minister say that the police were coming.

"Fuck the police!" he replied.

I was five-feet-nine. My boots added another inch or two at most. Although I was able to address the average male eye-to-eye, this fellow was at least six-feet-five. And he was big. He wore a leather vest and had his hair cut in a Mohawk style. Even from the back, he was intimidating and I was scared. I knew that my backup would be at least five to 10 minutes away but as I was there and in a police uniform, I was expected to do something. To this day, I am not sure what prompted me to approach the fellow the way I did. I walked up behind him and reached up, putting my hand on his shoulder. I looked him square in the eye.

"You're not going to 'fuck' any police officer today," I said.

He probably could have taken me out with one swipe of one of his massive arms, but instead he looked at me and started to laugh. To my relief, he had a sense of humour.

I asked his name.

"Alex," he said.

The liquor on Alex's breath and his overall hostility told me that he had been drinking.

I explained to Alex that he could not stay at the mission as the minister had asked him to leave, but I told him that he was welcome to "sleep it off" in cells and that I would let him out once he had sobered up. The giant agreed and dutifully followed me to the police car, head hung low where he squeezed himself into the back seat. I continued to treat him kindly and with respect and in return Alex gave me no problems during the booking-in process. And, as promised, later that day I went to the cellblock to release him.

Alex was new in town and as the summer progressed, he became quite well known to most of the police officers at my detachment. He had no family in the area and had wandered into our community for who knows what reason. He was just hanging around. He was often arrested for fighting or causing a disturbance, or just for being drunk in a public place. Alex was known to give the male officers a good fight every time he was arrested. Each time I ran into Alex in cells, I would ask him what he had done to be there.

His usual response was to hang his head, look at me rather sheepishly, and say "I'm sorry. I was bad."

He always seemed to be genuinely remorseful. I felt sorry for Alex and tried my best to connect him with the agencies in town that could help him. I wasn't looking for a reward, but it turned out that there were was an unexpected benefit that came out of how I treated Alex.

Late that same summer, the city began the process of clearing out a block of old homes to create space for a new development. Just one home remained, propped up on blocks, ready to be moved. Given that the evenings were starting to get cold, some of the local transients decided to use this old house to bunk in for the night. Although they were technically trespassing, a number of us at the detachment felt that as they were off the streets, out of harm's way and not causing any problems. There was no reason to bother them. Anyways, no one had even complained about their presence there. But during one night shift, I heard my trainer advise our dispatcher that he was going to check the derelict house and roust out the transients. I naturally started heading in that direction in case there were any problems. It didn't take long before my trainer called for backup which was a rare event for him. Being the closest car, I responded and advised that I was on my way. I could practically hear my trainer's sigh of disappointment, learning that it was me responding, rather than one of the guys.

I pulled up to the scene and entered the house on foot, working my way through piles of garbage. I headed towards the commotion which turned out to be coming from a back bedroom. When I entered the room, I could see shadows of about 10 people in sleeping bags cowering against the walls. Meanwhile, my trainer and Alex were in the middle of the room, squaring off to do battle. Alex towered over my trainer who had his hands balled into fists, ready to take Alex on with just his bare hands. From the doorway, I calmly asked Alex what was going on. He turned around, recognizing me in an instant. He immediately hung his head and apologized to me. Briefly, he looked back towards my trainer before following me out of the house to my police car. We left my trainer standing there in that room, jaw hung open. I often wonder how he managed to properly compose himself in front of all those witnesses in sleeping bags. He never did thank me for helping him out of what could have been a very bad situation.

After that night, I did not see Alex again. I presume he either went home or moved on to another community. However, the life changing lesson he taught me has stayed with me throughout my career. That summer, I learned that I could never approach my work like one of the guys. I had to do police work my own way, a female way. This approach proved to be much more effective for me than traditional strong-arm tactics. I also learned that when I treated people with respect, they would in turn treat me with respect and if I was honest with people, they trusted me. I often think of Alex and the lessons I learned through my dealings with him. He certainly was no Prince Charming, but he did influence my policing style which positively impacted my career. For that I owe him debt of gratitude.

THE KICK IN
Sergeant Andrea Hooper Rhodes (Ret.)

I graduated from Depot in July 1983. The day after the ceremony, I started my journey from Regina, Saskatchewan to my first posting in Oshawa, Ontario. I'd loaded all of my worldly possession into a brand new Plymouth Sundance. It was my first car paid for by my first loan and driven with the authority of a drivers license that I had acquired only a year earlier in my hometown of Whitehorse, Yukon.

Eager to soak up every experience I could, I took the scenic route east through the United States. I drove through Chicago at rush hour and saw the famous factories of Detroit before finally re-entering Canada. I arrived in Oshawa in the dead of night, armed with only the street address of my new detachment.

I found a motel to crash in for the night. The place was a dive but I was too tired to care. The next morning, despite the fact that I had a few days before I was expected to report for duty, I decided to check out my new detachment.

Of course, in my case, "police detachment" was a metaphor of sorts. Ontario was (and still is today) a non-contract province. This meant that everyday policing matters were dealt with either by small municipal police departments spread around the province or the Ontario Provincial Police. The role of the RCMP in Ontario was generally restricted to enforcing federal statutes other than the Criminal Code of Canada and conducting larger long-term investigations. I knew that by virtue of my post, I would not be driving a marked police car nor would I likely be wearing a uniform. In essence, I would not be doing a lot of what I had been taught at Depot.

After making a few enquiries, I discovered that my detachment was actually a leased office space located on the sixth floor at Oshawa City Hall. As I rode the elevator, I reflected that my experience in my first posting would be quite different from those of many of my troop mates who had been posted to contract policing positions around Canada.

I exited the elevator on the sixth floor and knocked on a nondescript door. After a few moments, when no one answered, I pounded harder. Eventually, I heard the lock disengaging. The door opened slowly and I was greeted by a lovely lady who turned out to be the detachment clerk. She introduced me to the sergeant in charge and a few of the members working in the office. No one was in uniform. I was also introduced to my assigned trainer. Having just completed an undercover project, he did not look anything like the typical tall, broad shouldered, clean shaven, square-jawed Mountie you might see in an Arnold Friberg painting. Like me, he was only twenty-one years old and looked to be about 120 pounds. At about five foot five, he was no taller than me. I thought he resembled a hardened, long-term member of an outlaw motorcycle gang. He was also not in uniform.

My new sergeant suggested that since I had dropped into the office, I might as well start working right away. My scheduled leave hours, he said, could be banked for another time. I wasn't so sure about that but I'd learned at Depot that it is always a good idea to follow your supervisor's advise, so I agreed.

I learned that I would be working with the detachment's Joint Operations Drug Section during the six months of my recruit field training. I met the other members of the section who besides my trainer included a couple of seasoned RCMP Drug Section members, and a member from a local police force who looked suspiciously like Han Solo's sidekick in *Star Wars*.

It just so happened that on this particular day, my team was executing a search warrant at the residence of a local drug dealer. During the briefing, they made it sound fairly routine as far as search warrants go. It was routine, except for one thing: information was received that the target of the search warrant kept a very large and exotic snake in his residence. It was believed that the snake was likely to be loose somewhere inside the home. This was not good news, as I was terrified of snakes.

Normally, a new recruit would be very excited to go on her first search warrant or "kick in." However, in this case, all I could think of was what would happen if I encountered the snake. Did I mention that I really hated snakes? Of course, I kept my concerns to myself. I was the new recruit and had to make a good impression.

My team armed me with a detachment "loaner pistol," which at the time was a six shot Smith & Wesson .38 Special snub nose revolver. In training, we had often joked that this pistol made even the broad side of a barn appear to be a particularly small target. I wondered how much accuracy I would have if had to use it.

When we arrived at the suspect's town house, it was decided that the smallest person on the team would enter first through an open kitchen window and let the rest of the team inside through a side door. I was not shocked when that person turned out to be me.

Without any discussion on the matter, I was unceremoniously hoisted up to the kitchen window. I squeezed myself through the small opening and stepped into a thankfully empty kitchen sink. We believed the residence to temporarily vacant and free of any four-legged variety of animals. But it was the zero-legged ones I was worried about. All I could think about was being the main course of a large reptile. I wondered how my demise would be explained to my parents who was already not overly pleased with my choice of career.

I managed to crawl down from the counter and made my way through the kitchen and living room as quickly as I could. I hurried to the side door and turned the handle which, as if on cue, fell off in my hand. I suddenly felt like the expendable character in a B-rated horror movie and I wondered if it were possible to have a heart attack at the age of twenty-one.

When it was clear our initial entry plan had gone sideways, the team wasted no time in gaining entry into the residence by kicking in the cheap door. What a relief. My trainer immediately directed me to conduct a search of the kitchen. As I poked around the tiny kitchen I was surprised at how clean it was. I breathed a sigh of relief, there didn't seem to be anywhere large enough for a snake to hide. I started my search in the lower cupboards and drawers, and began making my way around the cramped space in a systematic manner.

It was not until I was halfway through my search that I suddenly got the feeling that I was being watched. I turned around in a flash and came face to face with a giant iguana, motionless and perched on top of the fridge. He gazed at me with one of his amber coloured eyes. His long tail was draped near the window I had crawled through only minutes before. To me, the creature looked like a shrunken dinosaur. Despite the fact that it felt like my heart was about to burst from my chest, I was able to keep any outward signs of fear in check. There was no shrieking or jumping and

I didn't pump it full of lead. I took a deep breath and ordered the iguana to stay on the fridge hoping it would follow direction. I hurriedly finished my search of the kitchen, occasionally checking over my shoulder for any signs of movement from my new friend. For the moment at least, it seemed that he had decided to stay put. Fine by me.

Having found nothing of evidentiary value in the kitchen, I proceeded into the living room to check on my trainer. I found him standing on the coffee table looking somewhat distressed. Apparently, a menagerie of exotic creatures including a rare lizard, several small species of snakes, and a number of tarantulas in cages had been found. But what was distressing my trainer was that several empty tarantula cages had been located amongst the occupied ones. There was no way of telling where the former occupants had gone. Perhaps they were laying in wait in the residence's shag carpeting. I felt for my trainer. I wasn't exactly fond of spiders, either.

After a moment or so, when nothing had leapt out from the shadows, gnashing fangs and spewing venom, my trainer stepped down from the coffee table and promptly assigned the rest of the living room search to me.

The room's centrepiece was a large aquarium which I estimated to hold approximately 100 gallons of water. Inside, I found a number of colourful and expensive looking fish. This drug dealer seemed to have a thing for exotic animals. Off to one side of the aquarium, and in the corner of the room, was a large tube television encased in a wooden frame and an Atari gaming console complete with attached controls dropped haphazardly on the floor nearby.

I noticed a large wooden box with a sliding lid located underneath the aquarium. It looked to be the perfect hiding spot for illicit drugs. I opened it gingerly, fearful that I might find some terrible insect or reptile inside. As it turned out, the box was the perfect hiding spot for nothing more than an aquarium pump and related paraphernalia. There was no insects, no reptiles and no drugs. I continued my search of the room, very aware that no one had located that snake.

I don't know why, but after a while of searching, I took another look at that aquarium. It was only then that I noticed that the water level had decreased significantly and the surrounding shag carpeting was soaked. To my horror, I discovered that while searching the area I had inadvertently disturbed the pump mechanism which was now slowly pumping water directly from the aquarium onto the living room floor. Those colourful fish were looking rather cramped in their ever shrinking habitat.

Hoping that I would not meet my demise through electrocution, I quickly ripped the pump's electrical plug from the wall. I peered into the quiet, murky water of the now half-full fish tank and could make out several fish eyes returning my gaze. I could see my career in Drug Section ending in a sea of algae and fish poop. However, my trainer seemed unconcerned when I reported the situation to him. Still, I made copious notes in preparation for what I expected to be an imminent, career ending lawsuit.

We left the suspect's residence empty handed but arrested him shortly after in the complex parking lot as he returned with a new stash of drugs.

After sending our suspect to the local municipal police detachment for processing, we contacted animal control officers to deal with his town house menagerie. Though we hadn't been able to find the snake, the animal control guys did. They didn't tell us where they had located it, and I think that none of us really wanted to know.

I returned to my motel that night feeling that if my first day on the job was any indication of what was to come, I would be in for a very interesting and unconventional career. Turns out, I was right.

CAPTAIN
Corporal Veronica S.E. Fox

It was a beautiful and frigid winter evening in Bamfield, British Columbia. Dressed head to toe in Canadian Coast Guard issue inclement weather gear, I directed my small rigid hull inflatable vessel along a narrow channel. I flipped up the visor on my orange helmet and, enjoying the beauty around me, absently whistled a tune.

"What are you doing!?" exclaimed my companion. "You'll whistle up a storm!"

That winter of 2013, I was sent to be a student on the Canadian Coast Guard's Rigid Hull Inflatable Operator Training (RHIOT) course as a member of the RCMP. RHIOT School runs every fall and winter in the tiny community located on the south west coast of Vancouver Island. The combination of time of year and location allows participants to experience diverse and potentially unpredictable ocean environments.

I spent five of the most exhilarating days of my life at RHIOT School receiving training in search and rescue and extreme weather operations. I did things I had never dreamed of before I started. I dove under a capsized vessel to look for survivors, towed a ship that vastly dwarfed the one I was operating and re-boarded a vessel alone from the water with no ropes or ladders. I steered my vessel right up alongside another vessel travelling at high speed to transer personnel and equipment between ships, ran full-speed ahead in the pitch black of night with only distant beacons to guide me and maneuvered my tiny vessel through some of the roughest and most unpredictable waters in British Columbia.

My companion that evening was a seasoned veteran of the Canadian Coast Guard, an experienced mariner and talented musician who spent his days teaching charting, navigation and survival to wide-eyed students from various government organizations and his evenings mixing music or performing at local venues. Despite the fact that we had known each other for such a short period of time, he was someone I had a great deal of respect for. He and the other two male instructors on the course had treated me with fairness and respect. I was one of two women on the course but I was the only female student who was also a cop. Still, I inwardly rolled my eyes at the response I'd received for my whistling "faux pas." Mariners commonly hold superstitions about their vessels and the sea. Ironically, one of the most common is believing that having a woman aboard is bad luck. Apparently women are not considered strong enough, either emotionally or physically, to work on the water.

My first taste of marine patrol came in 2006 when a corporal at my detachment started up a summer patrol program in partnership with the Steveston office of the Department of Fisheries and Oceans located in Richmond, British Columbia. When I saw his email looking for volunteers, I was quick to reply. It sounded like an amazing opportunity.

I was barely off recruit field training when I first hit the waters as a guest aboard a Fisheries vessel. We patrolled the waters of the Fraser River in a 7.3 metre rigid hull inflatable vessel called the *Peregrine*. The Fisheries officers were very welcoming and willing to teach me all about water safety and navigation. We would check people fishing along the shoreline or cruising the river in private vessels. The Fisheries guys would handle all the fish stuff and I would deal with Criminal Code issues.

I spent the next few summers participating in these collaborative patrols and I loved it. I loved the interaction with the fishing community. I loved being out on the water. I loved contributing to conservation. During one patrol, we escorted a grey whale out of the Vancouver Harbour. It was one of those moments where I could not believe they let me do this for pay.

In the fall of 2011, the Department of Fisheries and Oceans donated the *Peregrine* to the Richmond RCMP. There was no pomp and circumstance and no ceremony. One day they just handed over the keys, federal agency to federal agency. We were allowed to continue using their moorage until we made other arrangements. A small group of us from the detachment took RCMP approved courses on basic and then advanced marine navigation. We traded out the Fisheries decals for the buffalo logo of the RCMP and the next summer, we hit the waters. Schoolchildren helped us pick a new name for our vessel: The *Fraser Guardian*. It wasn't until a couple years later that I learned changing the name of a vessel is considered by some mariners to be bad luck.

I patrolled the waters of the Fraser River aboard the *Fraser Guardian* as a captain for two years before going to RHIOT School. I was the only female member at my detachment who volunteered for the part-time job and during those years I encountered only a handful of other female captains out on the water. Every shift, I would captain the *Fraser Guardian* with two or three regular members or auxiliary constables aboard. The *Fraser Guardian* is a beautiful vessel. She has powerful twin outboard motors, bright police decals and a blue strobe light bar mounted on the wheelhouse. Aboard her, we performed many different duties including conducting safety checks of vessels in the river and nearby Strait of Georgia and attending marine calls for service and community events.

In my mind, the best word to describe working on the water is "treacherous." Operating a vessel is not at all like driving a car. For the captain, there is a lot to think about: Water currents, tides, the speed and direction of your vessel, the estimated speed and direction of other vessels, floating hazards, submerged hazards, and the list goes on. On the water, every decision has consequences, and that's just when we're talking about navigation. I soon learned that for a police officer pulling double duty as a captain, things could be even more complicated. Besides being concerned about the river current, I had to be alert to the fact that any vessel we stopped might be carrying something illegal. I had to not only keep an eye on the approaching barge, but also mind the hands of the boat operator we were currently dealing with. As captain, I was keenly aware that I was responsible for the safety of not only everyone aboard my own vessel, but those we checked in the course of our duties as well. It was a responsibility I took very seriously. Often, I found myself giving direction to members who were senior to me in service, age or both. But that was the way it was—the captain's word was law out on the water, because safety was paramount.

My crew, and members of other professional organizations, were hardly ever an issue. However, I found that some civilian mariners we encountered seemed to have difficulty following my direction. A good example, was a man who took his seven year old son fishing in a rubber dinghy. When conducting checks in the Fraser River, my common practice was to point the bow of the *Fraser Guardian* upstream and have the vessel being checked come alongside. The operator would be given two lines: one for the bow and one for the stern. After they had looped the ropes around their deck cleats, the other boat operator was directed to cut their engine and I took over navigation for both vessels using the *Fraser Guardian*'s twin engines. At least that was how it was supposed to work when people followed directions.

With the father and son in the dinghy, my crew tossed the man two lines and I asked him to secure his vessel alongside mine. The son immediately ran the rope through the lashing on the dinghy and handed it back to my crew, securing our sterns together. But the father just sat there in the bow, staring up at me from behind dark sunglasses, mouth slightly agape. I asked him again to secure his bow to mine. Instead, he placed the loose rope in his lap and started talking to my crew. That was when things literally went sideways. Caught in the swift current of the river, the man's unsecured bow pulled away from mine and his dinghy pivoted at the stern where his son had dutifully fastened our vessels together. The father made a mad scramble for the coils of rope that were quickly disappearing from his lap but it was too late. The rope trailed into the water as his dinghy completed its 180 degree turn. I had a terrifying vision of his son, him and his feeble little dinghy getting sucked into my engines, so I cut power. Yet this meant the *Fraser Guardian* was now being swept backwards with the dinghy, as the river's current dragged us toward a large barge docked downstream. My crew was switched on and freed the boats right away so I could safely re-engage the engines. It all worked out, but that day I learned that if I wanted to be captain, I could not afford to be nice. It just was not worth the risk.

I found it an ongoing struggle to overcome the way society was telling me to behave as a woman:

"Why are you such a ballbuster?"

"Be sure you don't bulk up. No one likes a woman with muscles."

"You're too independent."

"Don't be such a bitch."

A whistling woman and a crowing hen, are neither good for God nor men.

It did not happen overnight, but slowly I learned to give direction and orders rather than make suggestions. I replaced "would you mind..?" with "you're going to..." and I stopped saying please. I learned to be "rude." I found a new confidence on the water and even changed my approach to some land-based files as well. And that was a good thing, because it better prepared me for what was to come.

It was a hot July day in 2012 and I was in the office enjoying a late lunch with some teammates when our dispatcher alerted us that a floatplane had just made an emergency landing on the Fraser River near Gary Point Park in Steveston. My team and I looked at each other from across the table. This was it. I got on the radio advising dispatch that I would be heading down to the boathouse to fire up the *Fraser Guardian*. My two teammates (now my crew) raced with me to the detachment parking lot.

The three of us took one marked police car with me riding in back. On the way to the boathouse we were updated that the pilot had stopped responding to air traffic control shortly before his floatplane had been observed landing in the river by park-goers. It now appeared that the pilot was okay and trying to take off again but was not having any luck.

The location where the plane had landed was a busy shipping channel, a thoroughfare for tugs and barges bringing goods up and down the river. This was not a location that vessels of any sort generally stopped or hung around in. It was definitely not a location from which floatplanes landed or took off. I knew we needed to get that floatplane out of there as soon as possible.

We made it to the boathouse in good time and climbed aboard the *Fraser Guardian*. My crew helped with a bare bones safety check and in record time we were off, speeding through the Steveston Harbour.

As we exited the harbour at the tip of Gary Point Park, the floatplane came into view. I headed straight for it. As we got closer, it became apparent that the floatplane dwarfed the *Fraser Guardian*. The river was rough and I was careful to keep sufficient distance away to prevent the plane's wings from clipping the wheelhouse.

My crew began trying to talk to the pilot. This did not go smoothly. It seemed that he could not hear us over the *Fraser Guardian's* engines and the noise of the river. He would pop his head out of the hatch on one side of the cockpit and shout at us before ducking back inside and turning over his engine. His floatplane had a single rear facing propeller that moved every time he tried to start the engine. I did my best to maneuver the *Fraser Guardian* in a bit closer so that my crew could communicate with the pilot. Meanwhile, I kept an eye on the current, our direction of travel, oncoming traffic from all directions, the ever changing distance between the floatplane and our vessel and, of course, those wings. The pilot kept turning the floatplane away from us and revving the engine. This was making navigation especially difficult and we soon realized that we could not get close enough to communicate. Even with use of the *Fraser Guardian's* loudhailer, we couldn't get him to head into Steveston Harbour. He was either ignoring us or couldn't hear our directions.

One of my crew came up with the great idea of getting the pilot's cell phone number. Once we did that, she called the pilot and told him to stop revving his engine. She then asked him what was wrong and why he had stopped communicating with air traffic control. The answer did not seem to shed any light on the issue. My crew member told the pilot that we needed to get him out of the shipping lane. I decided that we would tow him into Steveston Harbour. There was hardly any current there and the large public dock would easily accommodate his plane.

There was an argument about whose towline to use. The *Fraser Guardian* had a long length of floating rope designed specifically for towing, but the pilot wanted none of that. He insisted that we use his rope, and after tying it to the nose of his plane, threw the other end to my crew. The throw was short and the rope landed in the water and promptly sunk. I immediately cut the power but it was too late. Once again I found myself floating backwards down the Fraser River, this time with a bunch of rope coiled around my propellers. I've spent many an occasion since the incident beating myself up over this and I definitely was very hard on myself that day. But in retrospect, I suppose we had no way of forcing the use of our rope on the pilot as we could not reach the nose of the plane to tie it on ourselves. He certainly had been adamant that he wasn't going to. But still, where was that captain I had worked so hard to develop? Maybe if I had been more forceful. Maybe if I had been more commanding...

Still, I had a plan to get out of the predicament. I pulled the engines out of the water and advised my crew that someone was going to have to get wet. Bless them, they both immediately began stripping off gear. And that's when the angel in the skiff appeared seemingly out of nowhere. He said he was from the Harbour Authority and asked me if he could help. With one hand on his single outboard engine, he expertly maneuvered his tiny boat between the stern of my vessel and the nose of the plane.

After a few seconds I heard him say, "Okay! You're free!"

It was like a miracle and I was supremely convinced that he was not just talking about my vessel. When that rope was loosened from the engines of the *Fraser Guardian*, I felt it loosen from me as well, and somewhere inside, the Captain woke up. I might have been stuck using the pilot's rope, but I was taking charge. This floatplane was going to port. Immediately.

We were soon underway, floatplane in tow. I brought us around and headed upstream towards Steveston Harbour, but my crew member, still on the phone with the pilot, relayed that he wanted us to continue past the harbour to some port I had never heard of. He was adamant it was just a few knots up the river. This time, there was no argument. This time, the Captain was steadfast. We were going to Steveston Harbour and nowhere else.

Suddenly, I heard the unmistakable sound of an aircraft engine springing to life.

"He's starting the engine! He's starting the engine!" shouted my crew member in the stern.

That moment remains the second most terrifying experience I've had on the job. I still shudder just thinking of it.

Everything happened at once and in a split instant. I cut forward thrust, creating some slack in the towline. My crew member in the bow ran past me towards the stern, reaching for the knife in his duty belt. I reached up and blasted the sirens. Meanwhile, my crew member shouted commands to the pilot over the phone.

One hand on the wheel, I looked back to make sure I would know the exact moment we were cut free of the towline so I could get us out of there. But the floatplane engine stopped just as suddenly as it had started. For a brief moment, everything paused. Through the cockpit's windshield I could see a broad smile. The pilot was laughing.

"Don't do that again," my crew member said firmly into the phone.

I felt a sudden buildup of emotion. I had no idea why anyone would want to endanger their own life and the lives of three Mounties attempting to help them. But I do know the rage I felt when I saw the bemusement on his face.

My legs and hands had started shaking, but I knew this was not the time. There was still a job to do. As I pulled us around again and headed into the harbour, my crew member gave the pilot a safety lecture that wiped that smile right off his face.

Several minutes later, I pulled us in to the dock which was thankfully unoccupied, allowing ample room to maneuver. We were able to secure the floatplane and deal with the pilot. And that was that. A cute little story appeared briefly on the website of a local media agency alongside a photograph taken from Gary Point Park by a member of the public. The picture was grainy and had been taken from too far away. No one had any idea about what had really happened out there on the water.

That day changed me. From that point on, I fully embraced the role of Captain and made sure I was never again stifled by anyone. I like the Captain. She's steely and tough and knows what she wants. And she whistles.

Back in Bamfield, the setting sun painted the heavens and cast a cheery red glow on the water as it sat low on the horizon. A red sky at sunset is considered good luck amongst mariners. Gazing out across the seemingly endless waves of the Pacific, I asked my instructor for our heading.

"You choose," he said. "You're Captain."

PART II

BALANCE

ADAM'S STORY – SOMETIMES YOU NEVER FORGET A NAME
Sergeant Stephanie Ashton

Shortly after I returned to police work following the birth of my first son, I became involved in a situation that was very difficult to deal with. I went home after one particular night shift in July of 1999 feeling angry, sad and very much affected by what I had experienced. Adam's story is difficult for me to tell.

In 1996, I left a career in journalism that I loved to join the Royal Canadian Mounted Police. I was twenty-eight years old and eager to take on the challenges that a career in policing promised. At my first posting in the Lower Mainland of British Columbia, I worked long, hard hours and balanced my new role as a police officer with my existing friendships and relationships. I believed that policing was not only a job, it was a lifestyle. When I joined the Force, I stopped being simply a wife and friend. I was now a *cop*, a wife and friend. The way in which I chose to define myself did not change until January 1999 when I took on the most important role of my life: being a mother.

My children are the joy of my life and being their mother has been more important to me than anything else I've done. My choice to have children in no way meant that I stopped doing the best job I could as a police officer. It just meant that my priorities in life needed to change. When I first became a mother, it was no easy task to shift from focusing primarily on myself, the job and my responsibilities as a police officer, to putting the needs of my children first. But I made a conscious commitment to invest myself in my children. I'm sure most mothers would agree that once you make the choice to give birth or adopt a child it becomes a balancing act between maintaining your identity as an individual and fulfilling your role as a mother. The children absolutely take priority. You rarely, if ever, put yourself first.

After my first son was born, I was fortunate enough to be able to spend six blissful months at home bonding with him. When my time at home with him came to an end, I returned to shift work.

I put a conscious effort into balancing my role as a police officer with my role as a mother. Instead of spending my lunch breaks bonding with teammates over restaurant meals, I would drive home, strip off my body armour and gun belt, and spend a few minutes with my baby before hitting the road once again. It was a new and difficult experience to be missing him while simultaneously meeting the needs of others in the community. I dealt with many different situations where families and small children were impacted by crime with new insights from my experiences as a mother.

On the night of the incident, I had been back to work for only five shifts. It was July and I anticipated an evening filled with the activities I'd come to expect from a summer night shift at my detachment: Chasing teens out of the parks and pouring out their beer, resolving family disputes, catching car thieves and purse snatchers and sometimes dealing with some significantly more serious issues. Generally speaking, nights in the city were busy and interesting.

At around 2:00 a.m., my dispatcher asked me to respond to a suspicious circumstance. A couple living in an apartment building had called 9-1-1 to report that they'd been hearing a baby crying for the past three hours. Apparently the couple hadn't realized until just prior to their phone call that the noise had been coming from outside. It was unseasonably cold that July.

Three other officers were dispatched along with me to search for the baby. I patrolled the neighbourhood with my windows rolled down hoping I'd be able to hear the crying and follow it to its source. I zipped up my patrol jacket against the cold night air.

My partners and I found a pickup truck tucked in behind an apartment building. When I pulled up, I could just make out the sound of a baby crying weakly. I got out of my patrol car and looked into the truck bed. Inside, I found two sleeping adults who reeked of booze and a baby, wearing nothing but a sleeper, sitting in a vibrating chair for infants.

The baby was tiny, very new, and clearly distressed. I estimated his age to be just two months old. I saw a little blanket at his feet that he had probably kicked off earlier as he'd begun to cry and move around. There was also a diaper bag.

I followed my instincts and immediately reached inside the truck bed and pulled that baby out of there. I grabbed his blanket and swaddled the child inside my patrol jacket to warm him. Although I've always maintained the view that babies should not be cuddled next to gun belts and body armour, warming him up was the primary goal. I was thankful that it was summer. I knew this would have been a different type of call if it had been any other season.

Once I was able to calm him a bit, I took that diaper bag and changed his diaper right there in the back seat of my patrol car. This was a place I'd put angry drunks and bloodied bar patrons fresh from a fight. It was a place where I'd had to clean up the blood and vomit of teenagers and adults who had overindulged or made bad choices. This was no place for a newborn. But his diaper was soaked, and that wasn't helping my efforts to warm him. I found what I had to do particularly saddening in part because I knew that at that very moment, my own baby was at home sleeping, clean, cuddled up and warm.

I found a bottle of formula inside the diaper bag and stuck it under my arm in an attempt to warm it. I cranked the heat in my car and sat in the front with the baby in my arms. I asked our dispatcher to call for a social worker.

While I was busy with the baby, the other police officers did their best to rouse the man and woman sleeping in the back of the pickup truck. The two, who we later learned were the infant's aunt and her boyfriend, were so drunk that they had to be dragged out of the back of the truck, put into police cars, and driven to the detachment to sober up.

It took almost a half hour for the social worker to make it to my location. By that time, my partners back at the detachment had roused the adults enough to learn the baby's name: Adam. It was confirmed that baby Adam was eight weeks old. His aunt had assumed custody of him because his mother was addicted to heroin and unable to meet his needs. We learned that Adam was receiving treatment for the residual effects of his mother's drug use during her pregnancy.

Sitting alone with Adam in my patrol car gave me plenty of time to think. I thought about how much I missed my baby who I knew was safe at home sleeping in his warm bed. I knew that any potential cry would be answered quickly by family. It broke my heart to think that Adam was lacking the very basics that every child should have. I also thought about one of the other police officers who had attended the call with me. I knew that he and his wife had been unsuccessful in conceiving their own child and had just recently started the adoption process. Adam's circumstances seemed even more unfair when I thought about how much better off he would be with that other officer and his wife.

When I turned Adam over to the social worker, I helped buckle him into a car seat. I covered him with his blanket and put his diaper bag beside him. I was afraid for Adam. Who knew what his future held? I went back to the noisy party complaints and thefts from vehicles that were waiting in our dispatch queue knowing that I'd probably never see him again.

Later, near the end of the shift, I parked my patrol car in a local park to write up some reports. I was joined by the other officers who had been with me when we found Adam. We were all moved by this incident and took a few moments to talk about how sad it was. That's what cops do so they can move on and deal with the issues and problems of countless others who need their help. After all the reports were written and the sun was up, we all went home. I hugged my son a little longer than usual before heading to bed. No body armour or gun in sight.

About three months later, one of the police officers who had been at Adam's rescue told me that he had just come from a call at the aunt's house. Police had been called to the residence after the aunt had gotten into a fight with her boyfriend. Recognizing the family name, the police officer had made it a point of attending. When he entered the residence, he found the aunt, who had been drinking, and her boyfriend. He also found Adam, crying and back in that same vibrating chair. Phone calls to the social worker confirmed that Adam had been returned to the custody of his aunt. Ultimately, the police officer had to leave the child there.

It has been 16 years, and although I no longer work at my old detachment, I have not forgotten Adam. I remember his full name. I remember what he looked like as a baby of eight weeks, found in circumstances that no child should be forced to endure. I wonder what Adam looks like now. I hope that he is a healthy, happy young man like my son.

My firstborn is now a strapping six foot two tall young man with good grades and dreams of university. His brother will soon start Grade Eight and wants to be a robotics engineer. I can only hope that Adam has been equally free to strive for his dreams. I know that even in families where there is substance abuse, there can be love. My hope for Adam is that he is in school, is being encouraged to reach his potential, and doesn't have to cry to get the love deserves.

Despite the many bad things I've seen in my role as a police officer, I've remained naively optimistic to this day, thanks in part, to my role as a mother. We all have our coping mechanisms and mine is the family I've created and the beautiful boys in whom I've chosen to invest my time and energy. Many years ago, I made a conscious decision to go from individual to mother. I managed to embrace this role while continuing in the profession that I love. I am not alone in this. Through the wonders of social media, I have been able to stay in touch with a number of young female police officers I've met through the years. I can see from their photos and comments posted online that they too have shifted their priorities and embraced motherhood. They have new babies and toddlers who are beautiful, happy and smiling. They look content. Each of us chose to embrace a non-traditional role when we became police officers. If the smiles in those photos say anything, it's that the choice to embrace motherhood has been just as fulfilling as our careers.

A CHANGE OF PLANS
Corporal Dawn Metallic

I was born the year the first women joined the RCMP, and grew up in Lis-tuguj, Québec, a Mig'maq community located on the border of Québec and New Brunswick. I was the youngest of seven children and attended a French Immersion program in Campbellton, New Brunswick. At the time, I didn't appreciate learning French but it benefited me later in life. My father passed away when I was fourteen years old. When it happened, my siblings had all long ago moved out of the family home. It was just my mom and I.

After high school, I attended Dalhousie University in Nova Scotia in hopes of becoming a social worker. It was there that I heard about the RCMP Summer Student Program. I applied and was accepted. After three weeks of training at the RCMP Training Academy (Depot) in Regina, Sas-katchewan, I worked at the Lower Sackville Detachment in Nova Scotia for the summer. During that time, exposure to police training and shift work made me change career paths. I wanted to become a police officer.

I wrote the RCMP entrance exam but did not pass. I wrote it again the following year only to find that they had temporarily closed Depot and were not accepting any recruits. I returned to my home community for the summer.

The local tribal police had learned of my interest in policing and asked if I would work for them as an auxiliary constable on a part-time basis. I accepted their offer. After a few weeks, my *part*-time job turned into a *full*-time job. I worked over forty hours a week for a year and a half, assist-ing with all aspects of policing. There was talk about me receiving official training in the future so I could become a full member of the police force. But one afternoon, my co-worker and I responded to a domestic assault which involved a family that was very close to my own. After dealing with the situation, I knew it was time for me to move on. Policing was still what I wanted to do, but I no longer wanted to work in my own community.

When Depot re-opened, I wrote the RCMP exam for the third time. I remember the day I got the letter. I opened it in front of my mother.

"Ma, I passed! This is going to change my life."

I stayed on with the tribal police during my application process. I completed the paperwork as quickly as possible and even drove seven hours to Montreal to do the Physical Abilities Requirement Evaluation (PARE). I passed the physical test and stopped by the recruiting office to introduce myself. They congratulated me on passing the PARE before sharing the bad news: My eyesight didn't meet the requirements. I was devastated. I went to my hotel room and cried. After I calmed down, I found the courage to call my mother. She told me to come home and we would fix it. When I got home, I made an appointment with an ophthalmologist who gave me information on laser eye surgery. My mum found the money for it on the promise that I would pay her back. There were risks of side effects and laser eye surgery was expensive. Recruiting was clear that even if I fixed my vision, there were no guarantees I had be successful in the recruiting process. But I was determined and successful and five months later, I went to Depot.

Eight weeks into training, guess who showed up at Depot? Four of my former colleagues from the tribal police. In the late '90s and early 2000s First Nation stand-alone police services across Canada were mandated by Public Safety Canada to officially train all their police officers at an accredited police academy, and the Listuguj Police Department had selected Depot. My friends joined a regular troop but wore their own uniforms. After graduation, they returned to police their home community. It was nice having them there and I felt less homesick. Like everyone else, there were days when I wanted to pack up and leave.

I remember running on the treadmill in the gym, staring at the EXIT sign, thinking to myself, *I hate running. I'm not being paid to be here. Why am I here? I should just leave.*

But then I would think of my mom. If I left training there was no way in hell I could ever face her again. She'd be too disappointed. My mom was a woman of few words. She had never said that I *had* to become a Mountie, but I knew that I would bring shame upon her if I just packed up and quit. So I stayed and thought of my mother and the pride and joy I could bring her.

During my staffing interview at Depot I asked to be posted to the Maritimes. When they asked why, I explained that I was Mig'maq and wanted to work in a Mig'maq community. I also spoke French which would be an asset in the Maritimes.

They said, "Chances are, you are going to British Columbia. You can work on a reserve there."

That comment left a bad taste in my mouth. This person clearly had the erroneous belief that all Aboriginal communities were alike. Little did they know that I knew the Officer in Charge of Aboriginal policing in Ottawa and Montreal. I made a few phone calls. I strongly felt that I would better represent the RCMP if I was posted back east. A few weeks later, I received my posting to Nova Scotia. I don't know if staffing had a change of heart of if someone changed it for them.

I graduated from Depot close to Christmas. My family didn't have the money to fly out to Regina so just my mother attended, thanks to the generous assistance of the chief in our community. All my troop mates had large groups of family and friends at grad, but I didn't feel bad. The most important person in my life was there, and that was all I needed.

After graduation, I flew home on the same flight as my mother. We flew through a snowstorm and I thought for sure we were going to crash.

All I kept thinking was, *Great, I finally accomplish something in my life and now I am going to die in a plane crash.*

Thank God we landed safely. I had a few days at home before the movers arrived to pack up my belongings. I said goodbye to my mother and took the train to my first posting in Nova Scotia.

I was thrilled to be back in Nova Scotia, it was my second home. I had attended university in Halifax and knew the province. I was familiar with all the Mig'maq communities and understood the language. I was a six hour drive from my home community. I was living the dream.

A few months later, I started dating another member of the RCMP who worked in a neighbouring detachment. He was originally from Montreal and expressed his interest in returning to Québec someday. I did not think too much about where our relationship was going as we had different career interests. He wanted to go to back to Montreal and I was not leaving Nova Scotia. We dated for a few years, then September 11th happened. He was soon offered a transfer to Toronto and asked if I would go with him. Staffing said that I could transfer with him as long as we got married! He proposed and two weeks later we got married. It was just before Christmas.

My husband and I settled in the big city of Toronto and staffing found me a job at the Toronto Airport Detachment. For the first three months, I had huge regrets. I wondered if I had made a mistake with my career. The work was not the same and the people were not the same. I was not in uniform anymore and didn't drive a police car. The RCMP was not the police of jurisdiction and I had to commute sixty kilometres each way to work. I was further away from my family.

For a while, I went through the motions at work. I felt very disconnected from my First Nation roots. One day I attended an Aboriginal event in Toronto where I shared these feelings with a very wise corporal.

Her advice: "Dawn, you don't have to put people in jail to be a police officer. There are so many different ways you can contribute. You'll understand some day."

I thought about the advice. The corporal's words made me refocus on my priorities and where I wanted to be in this organization. I had to make a choice: return to Nova Scotia, a divorcee, or stay happily married and make my career work in Toronto.

As soon as I changed my attitude towards federal policing, things began to change. I made a phone call to National Aboriginal Policing Services in Ottawa and to Aboriginal Policing Services in Toronto and Montreal. A few months later, I was assisting these units with Aboriginal and recruiting events in Montreal, Ottawa, London and the James Bay area. I was on the RCMP's recruiting website and in their recruiting material. Both my immediate supervisor and the Officer in Charge of my detachment supported me in participating in Aboriginal events. They understood the importance of relationship building. My investigational skills paid off as well and I received an Award of Distinction for the first conspiracy conviction at Toronto Airport Detachment. Things were good.

Toronto Airport Detachment turned out to be the closest to police work I was going to get. We arrested drug importers on a daily basis, seized large quantities of drugs, obtained victim, witness and accused statements, photographed and fingerprinted prisoners and testified in court. It turned out to be a busy place and the years flew by.

A few years later, when my husband was transferred to Ottawa, I was transferred to protective policing where I maintained contact with National Aboriginal Policing Services. It was one of the ways for me to remain connected to the Aboriginal community.

After a few short months, I was seconded to National Aboriginal Policing Services (NAPS) for a project after which I returned to protective policing. Then in 2010, I received a phone call from the Officer in Charge of NAPS. He wanted to know if I would represent NAPS at the National Centre for Missing Persons & Unidentified Remains (NCMPUR). Missing and murdered Aboriginal women was a hot issue in Ottawa and across the country. The NCMPUR was tasked with developing a national website and database, police training programs and Canadian law enforcement best practices pertaining to missing persons and unidentified remains. I accepted the offer and became the team's Aboriginal liaison officer. My role was to ensure that there was an Aboriginal component to what was being created. I had now become a subject matter expert.

For four years I worked on numerous high level projects within the NCMPUR. The work did have its challenging moments but allowed me to reflect on how far I had come. I too had grown up in a First Nation community where I had been exposed to poverty, domestic violence, alcohol and drug addiction. As a young woman, I had been in an abusive relationship and it had taken me several years to find the courage to finally walk away. I felt honoured to be selected for my position on the NCMPUR.

I was recently promoted to corporal in NAPS. The work being done by our unit impacts the entire Force and communities across Canada. NAPS is working on several projects such as Missing and Murdered Aboriginal Women and Aboriginal Culture Awareness training for RCMP employees. We work with Aboriginal policing units in the provinces and territories to develop programs to build safer and healthier communities. We have run a hitchhiking awareness poster campaign and created public service announcements with Shania Twain and Jordan Tootoo. Even though I do not currently work directly in a First Nation community, I have found a way to give back to Aboriginal communities across Canada. I am currently assisting RCMP Recruiting with an Aboriginal mentorship program, communicating with Aboriginal RCMP applicants to encourage and keep them motivated as they progress through the lengthy application process. I had an RCMP member encourage me during my application process. If it was not for him, I would have probably joined another police service.

The wise corporal who shared her advice is now my chief superintendent. I attribute her motivating words to having helped me get to where

I am today. I am still married to the man I met in Nova Scotia and we have two healthy daughters. I am only halfway through my career. I am looking forward to the future, awaiting the challenges and experiences that are to come.

CAGED
Corporal Anette Martin (Ret.)

When I joined the RCMP in 1984, they handed me a very different dress uniform from the one men wore. I did not get the signature scarlet tunic, tailored to fit me perfectly. There were no shiny high browns or breeches with that iconic yellow stripe. Instead, I was issued a red blazer and white mock turtleneck that I wore with a knee-length skirt and black pumps. I got a special pillbox hat instead of a Stetson and I carried a purse. Everyone thought my female colleagues and I looked like flight attendants. While there was absolutely nothing wrong with being a flight attendant, we were cops, and wanted to look like cops. It might have been ten years since the first troop of women had been accepted by the RCMP, but we still had a long way to go.

I recently volunteered at a breast cancer fundraising event where I was happily surprised to run into an old colleague from my first posting in Surrey, British Columbia. We had not seen each other in ages, as is so often the case with Mounties. We spent a few brief moments catching up on a lifetime of occurrences. He was retired and working for a different police agency while I was leading a team of constables at another detachment. We spoke about our families. Anyone observing our interaction would have thought we had been life-long friends. But while Dave and I had indeed been friends for a long time, it had not actually started out that way.

During my early years with the RCMP, I found it difficult to fit in with my male counterparts. During those days, as was exemplified by our dress uniform, female members very much stood apart. There were no women in Dog Section or Emergency Response. No females had yet achieved the rank of inspector and women did not lead detachments. We were still the new kids on the block, and while some males were quite welcoming and accepting, others were not so keen to share their workplace with us.

My story with Dave went back to the summer of 1986. By that point, I had been working at Surrey Detachment for a little over two years. Dave, his friend Roger and I were all posted to the same General Duty Watch. In the early days, Dave and Roger were not too keen on working with me and they let me know this by making jokes or snide comments about police women when I was around. I overheard them say that one day they should let two female members handle a domestic on their own with no male police officer for backup. They laughed and described this as a likely "fatal experience." But the comments were not the hardest thing to deal with. One thing that really made me feel as if I did not belong on the team was that I was never invited to coffee, an important bonding activity for watch members. At first, I really took this to heart and I felt discouraged and unwelcome. It didn't seem fair. I had worked just as hard to get into the Force and graduate from Depot as the guys had but despite this, I couldn't seem to break into the culture. I saw myself as being isolated and unable to change my role in the Force and how I was viewed by my partners. I felt trapped, as if in a cage. But one day during that summer in 1986, I saw a chance to change my circumstances.

One afternoon, Dave and Roger got involved in a file of some urgency. To this day, I do not remember what the excitement was all about, but I do remember that they had been forced to go for a run (a very long and hard run) in the area of Crescent Beach in Surrey. They had chased a suspect a considerable distance from their police cars and onto the beach. The chase had ended at Thousand and One Steps which is a set of several staircases leading from the beach to a residential area. For Dave and Roger, being forced to climb the Thousand and One Steps after a foot chase was, undoubtedly, extremely exhausting. Understandably, once they reached the top, the guys requested a ride back to their vehicles. I was in the area, so I went to give them a lift.

I pulled up in my police car which was not much different from those driven by many police officers today. My car was a four door Crown Victoria with some very specific police modifications. Of course, it obviously had lights and sirens and flashy decals announcing that it was a police car, but one of the most important alterations was on the inside. The front and back areas of the police car were separated by a large sheet of plexiglass and metal referred to as a "silent patrolman." This special partition allowed for the transportation of persons under arrest in the back of the vehicle, while ensuring the safety of the police officers riding in the front.

The silent patrolman, along with the modified rear doors created a sort of portable cell that fully contained a prisoner until he was released by a police officer.

Even if one is not under arrest, riding in the back of a police car is not favourable. The back of a police car is cramped, uncomfortable, and not the cleanest of places. Police officers often arrest and transport drunk people who are sometimes known to vomit, urinate, or spit in the back. Even though the messes are routinely cleaned up, there is no denying the fact that the back seat of a police car is gross. However, it is sometimes a necessity of the job for a police officer to catch a ride in the back seat. In this case, either Roger or Dave would need to ride in the back while the other would have the privilege of riding "shotgun" in the front passenger seat.

But when I pulled up, Roger leaned in the passenger window and said, "No way! I'm not getting into the front with a female member!"

Without another word, Roger jumped into the back along with Dave and pulled the door closed. This is when the idea came to me.

I think the guys realized that they had made a mistake almost immediately after closing their doors. I couldn't help but giggle as I slammed the window in the silent patrolman shut. I ignored their shouts to let them out. I'd decided that it was their turn to feel trapped by circumstances.

It was quite hot that day and back then, police vehicles didn't have air conditioning. Dave and Roger soon began sweating in the back seat. I decided to make them sweat some more and took a detour on the way back to their cars. My first stop was the fire hall located in the Crescent Beach area. I went in and asked the firefighters to come out so I could show them something in my patrol vehicle. At that time in the Lower Mainland, policemen and firemen had a long-standing, friendly and professional rivalry, so when the guys from the fire hall saw Dave and Roger imprisoned in the back seat of my police car, they laughed at them. After this, I then paraded my captive colleagues to the other fire hall across town. More firefighters came out and laughed. By the time I finally drove them back to their cars, Dave and Roger's formerly angry complaints were now laced with laughter. I'd made my point, and they knew it.

In the days, months and years that followed, it was clear that I had earned the respect of Dave and Roger as well as many others on the job. I was now invited to coffee and my team and I shared the sense of camaraderie I had yearned for when I first joined the Force. When his second child was born, Roger and his wife asked me to be their new son's godmother. And now, years later at a charity event, I was able to joke and laugh with Dave about my bold move on that hot summer in 1986.

Many things have changed since my early years in the Force. Women are more accepted as police officers by both the public and their male peers and I was long ago issued with the standard modern red serge that today, all Mounties (both male and female) wear with pride. My old red blazer is a thing of the past, a museum piece that I sometimes bring into the office to show my wide-eyed contemporaries.

"You mean, when you joined the Force, you didn't get a regular serge like the guys?" people ask when I show them my old kit.

"Things weren't always like they are now," I tell them.

I am proud to be a Mountie, but it is not just my new uniform that makes me feel this way. On that day so many years ago, I found the strength inside to not only earn the respect of my peers, but also prove to myself my ability to change my own circumstances, to escape the confines of my cage, and to embrace my role in a career unlike any other.

LITTLE BRANDAN – FOREVER MY LITTLE HERO
Sergeant Regina A. Marini

I first met "Little" Brandan one brisk autumn afternoon when I was called to a residence following a 9-1-1 call reporting a male passed out in a backyard.

I attended the scene. It was a residential neighbourhood where it was unusual to find someone passed out in the open. The home owner who had called the police showed me to his unfenced backyard where I observed a very skinny male, face down in the grass. He was wearing jeans and a t-shirt. Next to him was a small boy, no more than six years of age. He was pulling on the man's arm, begging him to get up. I tried to rouse the man. The obvious odour of liquor on his breath told me he had been drinking excessively.

The little boy started crying and I confirmed that this was his father.

"Please get up, Dad," he begged. "The cops are here."

I asked the little boy what his name was.

"Brandan," he told me.

I told Brandan that I was going to give his dad a good and safe place to sleep and recover. I told him that everything was going to be okay. With a maturity beyond his years, Brandan wiped away his tears and helped me get his father to his feet. Brandan and I walked his father over to my police car, supporting him on either side.

Little Brandan helped me put his father in the back of my police car. The father roused briefly but soon settled in to sleep it off in my back seat. Meanwhile, Brandan climbed into the passenger seat. We sat in the front for a bit and talked. Brandan told me his name, his father's name and the address where he said they lived along with his mother. I realized that Brandan lived in a neighbourhood well known to the members of our detachment. Regrettably, police were often called to Brandan's neighbourhood due to the high number of fights and domestic disturbances that occurred amongst the residents there.

Brandan struck me as very mature. He was street smart and quick to recognize that I was a friend who would help him. We formed an instant connection and I sensed that he knew that he could trust me. Brandan told me his mom was not home but that his adult sister lived nearby. He and I patrolled over to his sister's house with his dad still passed out in the back of my police car. I glanced over at Brandan. Tear stains remained on his cheeks. I was a school patrol officer and would regularly visit the schools in the area, delivering talks about bullying, vandalism or drugs. Often, I'd let kids climb around in my car, showing them how the lights, siren and loudspeaker worked. The kids always loved it and had a million questions. Sometimes I'd take a few for a spin around the block. Brandan, however, sat quietly looking out the window. He was clearly having a very different experience from most of the happy kids I dealt with at the schools.

When I dropped Brandan off with his sister, I again assured him that I would take good care of his father. I walked Brandan to the door where his big sister greeted us. I explained the situation to her. She did not seem surprised. She patted Brandan's head and guided him inside her home. I drove to the detachment and lodged Brandan's father into cells.

Over the next several months I got to know Brandan and his family as we were repeatedly called to the home for domestic disputes. His mom and dad had frequent arguments that quickly escalated into fights when alcohol was added to the mix. Their neighbours called police at least once a month. But every time I attended the family home, Brandan would come up to me and greet me with a smile.

"Hey, Lady Cop," he would say.

I think it was easier for him to call me that than pronounce my name. I must admit, I didn't mind.

"Have you come to get my dad?" he'd ask.

Often, we had. Sometimes Brandan's father was arrested and charged with something. Other times, he was just lodged in cells until he sobered up.

Frequently, when out on patrol, I would see Brandan riding his bicycle around his neighbourhood. He would wave at me and smile.

One day we got yet another call to attend Brandan's home. I attended with two colleagues, preparing for the usual. But this time, we found that Brandan's dad had beaten his mom pretty badly.

I stood in the residence's cramped living room with his mom while my partners dealt with the father. She was nursing a severe black eye. Brandan came over to chat with me as usual. Even under the terrible circumstances, he had a smile and friendly words for me.

My colleagues escorted Brandan's father to the main bedroom located just off the living room to allow him to collect some clothing. All of a sudden, Brandan's smile disappeared. Tugging on my uniform jacket, he looked at me with a serious face. It was obvious that Brandan had something he wanted to tell me. Something that he didn't want his mother to hear. I leaned over to listen to Brandan's important secret.

"Is my dad going to take his gun?" he whispered.

I ran to the bedroom yelling, "Gun!"

My quick thinking colleagues quickly shoved the father up against the wall. When we asked Little Brandan's father where the gun was, he pointed wordlessly to the bed. Sure enough, under the mattress we found a loaded handgun. Did he intend to use it? We will never know. But I can't think of a good reason someone would keep a loaded handgun under their mattress.

Despite his young age, Brandan knew that I needed to know the information about his father's gun. It was as if he instinctively knew it was a threat to the safety of him, his mother and the police who had shown up to his residence to help him. Brandan, like many other children growing up in similar circumstances, had learned very quickly about how to survive. It was sad. He really should have been innocently playing with toys and playmates. Instead, thanks to the alcohol, drugs and violence that were ever-present around him, he had lost a chance to enjoy such a childhood.

As for my colleagues and I, we learned an important lesson that day: Always listen to children. You never know what they may tell you. I also learned that you never know who you may encounter at any particular time who will end up having a lasting impact on your life. Brandan profoundly touched me that day and I've carried his memory all my life.

I heard Brandan's father moved out of town after serving his prison sentence. I later left also. Frequent transfers in and out of communities are often a reality for members of the RCMP. I lost touch with Brandan. But even after all these years, and especially after having two sons of my own, I often think about him and how he likely saved all our lives that day. I wish and pray each day that he managed to defy the odds and rise above the terrible conditions into which he was born through no choice of his own. There will always remain a special place in my heart for "Little Brandan"—My Little Hero.

DEFINING MOMENTS
Corporal Heather Dickinson

I was in my fourth year with service in the RCMP and working the night shift in Langley Traffic Section. As was typical with many winter nights in the Lower Mainland of British Columbia, it was raining. One night, I was accompanied by a very special ride-along: my dad.

My mom and dad had always been proud of the fact that I was a Mountie, but truth be told I do not think it was their first choice for my career. My husband and high school sweetheart Paul had also joined the RCMP. They were good with that, but their daughter? The idea of me working in a dangerous job as a police officer was a lot harder for them to embrace.

My parents live in Ontario, which is also my home province. When I was posted to Langley after graduating from Depot, we maintained close contact. Every Sunday I would call home to catch up on the week's happenings. My dad would get on the phone first. He wanted to know if Paul and I were healthy and safe. After confirming that everything was fine, he would quickly hand the phone over to my mom. I did not really talk to my dad about my work, though I knew he was interested in the policing world.

That winter, when my parents came out to BC for a visit, I thought a ride-along would be a great way to involve my dad in my career. Of course, a police officer today would probably not do this, but it was the '90s and things were a lot different back then.

The evening started off uneventfully. Then, approximately two hours into the shift, our dispatcher came over the radio advising all units that a police pursuit initiated by another police agency was coming into our area. We were advised that Matsqui Police (which later became the Abbotsford Police Department) were chasing a stolen van west into Langley.

I was in the area so I advised dispatch that I would block the road up ahead of the pursuit. I selected a location just north of the Greater Vancouver Zoo. We were basically out in the country, in the middle of nowhere.

Now, what I was about to do was very serious. As I had learned in training, roadblocks were dangerous and difficult to properly establish. And with regard to high-speed pursuits, I knew this to be possibly the most dangerous of all police activities. This was due to the risk to police and the public for of loss of life, serious personal injury or significant property damage.

I positioned my police vehicle across the roadway, turning on my emergency flashing lights and blaring the siren. Within minutes, Dad and I were able to see the flashing lights of approaching police vehicles in the distance as they traveled towards us along the country road.

The other police vehicles were pursing the stolen van directly towards our trap. I told my dad to get out of the car and directed him to wait on the shoulder at a safe distance. I was concerned that the stolen van would ram my police car which would put my dad's life at risk.

As the stolen van got closer, I noticed that it was not slowing down. It swerved and squeezed around my police vehicle, continuing down the road. I immediately pulled in behind it and was now the lead vehicle in the police pursuit.

I left my dad in the rain, standing on the shoulder of the roadway, watching me disappear into the distance.

The stolen van turned right onto a rural road which led to the on-ramp for the Trans-Canada Highway. As I followed onto the highway, I observed four police vehicles piling in behind me, all with lights flashing.

As we proceeded eastbound on the highway, I attempted to accelerate around the stolen van. I wanted to be in front of the vehicle to slow it down. The driver swerved the van but I was able to accelerate around him. I now watched the van in my rearview mirror as I decelerated while simultaneously matching his movements left and right to keep him from passing me. We continued on for what seemed like forever but I know in reality it was only a few minutes.

Suddenly the van made an abrupt left turn onto a restricted pull around lane! It was now very clear in my mind that the driver of the stolen van would do anything to avoid being apprehended.

I hit the brakes, yanked hard on the steering wheel and threw my car into a spin. I came around to face westbound just in time to see the other four police vehicles entering the pull around lane. I was now at the back of the pack. Not a place I was happy to be. The van pulled back onto the highway with five police vehicles in pursuit.

I listened to the updates from our dispatcher. The lead vehicle in the pursuit was from Matsqui Police and back then police officers did not have the capability to communicate directly with outside agencies over the radio. Instead, our dispatcher monitored the Matsqui Police channel and relayed information to us over the Langley channel. We were being provided with updates, but not in real time. I decided that I would move up, hoping I would be able to provide updates directly on the Langley channel. As luck would have it I found myself right behind the stolen van.

The pursuit was moving towards the more populated area of Surrey and a decision needed to be made soon to end this pursuit. We were advised by dispatch that there was no one in the area who could deploy a spike belt. I realized we would have to come up with another solution.

I decided to try and pull around the stolen van yet again. The driver did his best to prevent this from happening but after several back and forth tries I was able to accelerate past and take up a position in front of the stolen vehicle. The driver of the van tried to get around me. Back and forth we went as I attempted to slow him down. I now found myself updating on the radio while I matched his movements all while viewing the stolen van in my rearview mirror.

It was time to end this.

I noted that the Langley dog handler had moved his vehicle up beside the driver's side of the van while the remaining police vehicles brought up the rear. We now had the vehicle boxed in on three sides.

I advised the dog handler that we should hit our brakes on the count of three. He agreed.

"One! Two! Three!"

We hit the brakes. I braced for impact, fully expecting to be rear-ended by the van. Thankfully, I was not rammed. I jumped out of my police car and ran around to the passenger side of the stolen van just in time to see the fast approaching front end of a Matsqui Police vehicle. I had no time to think. I instinctively jumped into the air and found myself landing on the hood.

Yikes. That was close.

We arrested the driver, the lone occupant of the van. He had a Canada-wide warrant. We also found firearms in the vehicle.

After the scene had been secured, the Matsqui Police officer apologized for almost running me over.

"No harm, no foul," I told him. "It was totally my fault."

A good lesson learned for both of us.

I was still riding my adrenaline high when I was approached by a corporal. Truth be told, this corporal was not a fan of mine. But, I thought maybe he was on his way over to congratulate me on a job well done. As it turned out, that was wishful thinking. I could tell by the look on his face that he was not happy. Sure enough he began to lecture me, criticizing how I had handled myself during the pursuit. He talked about how risky and dangerous my actions had been. Of course he was right. But at the end of the day, I knew that police work was dangerous and had been prepared to take the risk to stop the suspect and ensure the safety of the public I served.

Once everything was reasonably under control, I remembered that I had left my dad at the side of the road! I made quick arrangements for another member to pick him up and bring him to me as I was busy with the investigation.

About 20 minutes later, I was back in my police car making my notes and speaking with my dispatcher on the radio channel reserved for longer conversation. My dispatcher congratulated me on the role I played in bringing the pursuit to a safe conclusion. I was flattered and honoured to hear her words. I felt privileged to be able to work with such an amazing group of police officers and support staff.

Shortly afterward, a police vehicle pulled up and out stepped my dad. He looked proud. On the ride over, he had heard my conversation with the dispatcher on the radio. My dad had always supported me and I had known he was proud of the work I did as a police officer, but this night became a defining moment in our relationship. Dad now understood that his "little girl" was a capable police officer.

Well, my dad was pretty wet from standing out in the rain. I asked him if he wanted me to take him back to our house.

"No!"

He wanted to stay and finish the shift. What a trooper!

Dad and I had a great time patrolling and attending calls for the rest of the shift. His presence in my patrol car was particularly special to both of us. In the 1950s my dad had considered joining the RCMP, but back then you could not be a hired as a married man. At the time, my dad had been engaged to my mom. He chose my mom over the RCMP. I am so grateful he did. It is strange how fate works. Although my dad never joined the RCMP, his daughter and son-in-law did. And now, here I was giving my dad a glimpse into the life he had once contemplated. My dad has told me that he has no regrets. He made the choice that was right for him and he knows I made the choice that was right for me.

As a result of Dad's ride-along-turned-adventure, our relationship changed. It was a defining moment. My dad still tells the story about the night his daughter left him at the side of the road, in the middle of no-where, in the pouring rain. Now my mom has a hard time getting the phone away from him when I call. We talk about policing and politics and stuff we never spoke of before. I have always valued my dad's opinion, but now he seeks out mine as well.

You just never know when one shift or one policing experience will result in a defining moment of change. It has happened to me on more than a few occasions.

CONFIRMATION
Corporal Veronica S.E. Fox

July 19, 2005 was sunny and hot. It was a normal summer day in the Lower Mainland of British Columbia, but it would turn out to be a very exciting one for me.

My phone rang around 1:00 p.m. I did not recognize the number, and picked up expecting to have to tell someone that I was not related to Michael J. Fox and that no, I didn't know his number (this had happened before). Instead, the stranger on the other end asked to speak to me by name.

The caller identified himself as a member of the RCMP. I am sure he told me his name, but I forgot it almost as soon as I heard it. "I have good news for you..." he said.

I nearly dropped the phone.

The voice on the other end of the phone advised me that I had been accepted by the RCMP. He gave me my troop assignment and told me I would be leaving for Depot in about three weeks.

I ran to get my day planner, calling down the hall to tell Mum the good news. We both cried with excitement. I was having a hard time believing it. It had been years of hard work. Now, after several hundred miles run, and almost as many volunteer hours logged, I was finally hearing the words I had dreamed of: "Welcome to the RCMP."

I returned to the phone and the voice on the other end began giving me details on what to expect in the next few weeks, and how to prepare for the upcoming six months of training. Before I hung up, Mum whispered a reminder for me to say thank you. I did. I still couldn't believe it.

It had been a long journey that had taken me from my initial application to the RCMP to the phone call I received that day. As with many other applicants to the Force, I had worked hard over the course of the several months that it took to complete the long and often challenging application process.

Getting into the RCMP was no easy task, nor should it have been. I had started my journey in June 2004. After attending an information session, I wrote the RCMP police aptitude test (RPAT). The test was comprehensive and lasted several hours. It touched on everything from math, logic and memory to English grammar and writing. I waited almost two months to receive my results via mail. Only after a confirmed pass was I able to submit my detailed and thorough application package which included some medical test results, documentation on past travel and employment, character references, and, most importantly, my test results from the Physical Ability Requirement Evaluation (PARE).

The PARE was a challenging obstacle course designed to ensure that applicants could meet the physical requirements of general duty policing. It was timed and included running up and down a flight of stairs, jumping over various obstacles, completion of a pushing and pulling task, and a controlled carry of a torso bag. This was one of my biggest challenges and required many personal hours of overall physical training.

In December 2004 and January 2005, I sat for two separate interviews with police officers. Over the next several months, while the RCMP conducted a thorough check of my background, I underwent full medical, dental, and psychological exams, obtained required certificates for typing and first aid, and retook the PARE as my old score had expired by that time.

Over the course of the entire application process, I worked full time, volunteered several hours a week at my neighbourhood community policing station, and as a member of a citizen's patrol organized by a local police detachment, participated in a sports club, and maintained a strict personal workout schedule. It had been many months of hard work. Now, a year and a month following my attendance at that first information session, I viewed the phone call I'd just received to be an indication that all that work had been worth it.

All things considered, I thought the day had turned out to be fairly fantastic. I had no idea it was about to get even better.

With only three weeks to go until I left home, and with a million things to do, I decided to head out right away to purchase some items I'd need for training. Top of the list: schedule a date with my hair stylist! Mum had some shopping to do as well so she came along.

We stopped at a drug store first. While we were purchasing a parking ticket, a young lady asked us for help with the ticket dispensing machine.

We spent several minutes helping her out and, as a result, were standing in the right place at the right time for what happened next.

As we were talking, I noticed a man run past us through the parking lot. This, in itself, was not very noteworthy. However, the fact that his pants appeared to be on fire definitely was. He was a pretty tall guy—at least six feet. He was wearing a black, puffy jacket which seemed out of place considering the warm weather. From his white basketball shorts he was trailing a large plume of red smoke. We all stopped mid-sentence to watch him run past. I remember at first being confused as to what I was seeing and then suddenly having this revelation—so that is what it looks like when a bank anti-theft dye pack goes off. I realized that this guy must have just ripped off the bank around the corner!

Everything happened so fast that I had no time to verbalize to Mum what I was thinking. Before I fully took in what had happened, I grabbed my cell phone and dialed 9-1-1. Leaving Mum and the young lady there, I ran after the thief. Having grown up in the community, I was fairly familiar with the area and did not think twice about following him into a nearby alleyway.

Meanwhile, on the phone, I was put through to an operator and told her what I had seen. I then began relaying to her the male's description, location and direction of travel. I really felt the adrenaline pumping. I won't lie, my hands were shaking. I had never chased a bank robber before.

The guy ran to the end of the lane and rounded the corner. I tried to keep him in sight but I had left some distance between us. As I came around the corner, I realized I'd lost him. But he had not been running that fast. Where could he have gone?

I looked around and spotted him through the window of the fast food restaurant on the corner. He was actually seated at a table counting the money right there in the restaurant. I was like, "Really?"

As I was updating the 9-1-1 operator, the bank robber suddenly came running out of the restaurant. For a brief moment in time we came face to face. Our eyes met. Here I was wearing a bright red T-shirt that said "Canada" on it, talking on a cell phone. I was sure he'd recognized me from the parking lot and realize I was calling the police.

Perhaps this story would be more exciting if I was able to say that I dropped the phone and judo-threw the bank robber over my shoulder, holding him until the police arrived. But in that brief moment I was fully aware that I was an unarmed civilian, untrained in anything other than rudimentary self-defense. I knew enough to know that bank robbers are often armed. This one seemed particularly unpredictable. As much as I might have wanted to, I knew that I possessed neither the tools nor the training to deal with something like this.

I looked around casually and shuffled my feet as I took a few steps away from the door. The operator asked me for an update.

I spoke to the operator as nonchalantly as possible, hoping the bank robber wouldn't realize I was on the phone with the cops, "Uh..." I said. "I guess ... Well, I'll see you on Kingsway, then ... Yeah. Right in front of the restaurant."

Amazingly, he turned and ran across the street. I followed him at a distance and saw him approach another male who had a young kid with him. To me, it looked like the bank robber was trying to convince this second male of something. The second guy was looking skeptical.

I updated the operator. "Where are your guys?" I asked.

Just then, I heard RCMP officers shouting from the lane. "Police! Get on the ground! Do it now!"

The skeptical-looking guy immediately dove for the ground, pulling his kid down with him without further urging. Meanwhile, the bank robber just stood there. The police officers had to apply some use of force tactics that I would later learn about at Depot, to get the male to comply with their orders. In the end, he was arrested without injury.

It took a bit for the officers to sort everything out. They let the second guy and the kid go when they determined that they were not involved. After robbing the bank, the suspect had actually stopped the man and his son to ask for a ride downtown in exchange for some money that "someone had spilled red paint on." *Sure...* The second guy was really quite understanding. He said he was okay with the police detaining him and knew they were just doing their jobs. His ten-year-old son described the experience to me as, "Cool." I was inclined to agree.

Over my nine years in the RCMP, I have had many different experiences. I've felt both the excitement of arriving first on scene at a crime in progress and the emotional low of delivering news of the death of a loved one. On some shifts, I have sat in the office for hours completing seemingly endless paperwork and on others I have missed meal breaks driving all night from call to call. I have sometimes worked long, arduous hours alone on complicated files and other times felt the shift fly by all too quickly while working closely with a partner or team I enjoyed and trusted.

Overall, my work as a Mountie has been both challenging and rewarding. Doing the job that we do means being willing to take on challenges, being able to take action when needed, and often deciding to run towards trouble even if everyone else is running away. This is why what happened on that sunny, summer day in July 2005 remains one of my best, favourite, and most self-defining memories. I would later draw on this memory to help me through the many challenging months of Depot training and the early years of my career. It was a confirmation for me that I was making the right choice and a start of what I hoped to be a long, exciting and rewarding career with the RCMP.

PEACEKEEPING JANE
Sergeant Jane Boissonneault

I arrived in East Timor in 2001, just two years after Indonesia had ended its bloody twenty-five year occupation of the tiny country located in Southeast Asia. The UN established a transitional administration while the world's newest country prepared to hold its first elections. Over 200,000 refugees had returned home to a country that could offer very little in the way of infrastructure and government services, so the UN had stepped in to fill the gap.

In support of the UN's mandate, the RCMP's International Peace Operations Branch sought out police officers with front line policing experience to help provide interim policing service and field training for members of the country's own new East Timor Police Service. Female police officers were being sought in particular. In East Timor, there had been no women in any kind of position of power or authority. There was, therefore, a big push to lead by example, showing the locals that women can do the job. Canada, known as one of the relatively few countries with fully trained, front-line female police officers was feeling the pressure to provide resources in this area. A friend of mine who was already associated with the mission contacted me and asked me if I would be interested in applying. At the time, I was an eight year member of the RCMP who had spent all my service working in rural communities in Saskatchewan. Growing up in Montreal, I had known I would be a Mountie since the age of ten. I had expected my policing career to take me far from home in Quebec; I just had not realized exactly *how* far from home I would end up.

I had heard stories about what to expect on a mission.

"If you think you're going to save the world, you'll be extremely disappointed."

"If you think they'll welcome you as some liberator, you're in for a shock."

Luckily, I had a friend who had participated in a couple UN missions and my conversations with him convinced me that it would be worthwhile to make the trip to East Timor. Sure, I probably wouldn't "change the world," but I might just improve the lives of a few individuals, and in my mind that would be well worth it. So when I stepped off that plane in Southeast Asia, it was my goal to make a positive impact at the personal level.

I worked alongside police officers from all over the world. Our goal as police trainers in East Timor was not much different than those of most police trainers in our own respective home countries. We were there to mentor new members of the East Timor Police Service as they learned the basics of conducting investigations within the rule of law and established traditions. Of course, there was no infrastructure to support our work. We had no guide books, no formal reporting and no official training resources. Not to mention, no common language. But somehow we managed, and it was an amazing experience being able to work within a culture different from my own.

While posted in Ermera District, I patrolled numerous small mountain villages along with other UN and East Timorese police officers. I drew on my RCMP training and experience in community policing and restorative justice to establish connections with the East Timorese community, an approach that was new to the local police and even some of my UN counterparts from other countries around the world. It was humbling and exciting to see how the "Canadian approach" to policing was picked up. It seemed to make the local police officers, and the communities for which they were responsible more comfortable with each other. Villagers were not used to having police work alongside them using the local restorative justice methods that had been around for hundreds of years. Before this, the police had only arrested people and taken them away. But in these tiny communities, where each villager relied on each other for survival, it made much more sense in many cases for a village chief to order a thief to make restitution to the victim of his crime than it did for a police officer to whisk the offender away to city jail.

It was on these village patrols that I got to know Maria. She was young, eager and a recent graduated member of the East Timor Police. She was just four foot nine, but what she lacked in height she made up in heart and determination. She was young, single and had several brothers who were also training to become police officers. Maria showed a great deal of interest in learning everything she could. She said she wanted to change the way the local communities felt about police, and female police officers specifically. I was honoured to mentor her as she grew in her role as a police officer in her home community.

I'd barely had a chance to familiarize myself with the East Timorese community and culture when I was transferred from patrol to the Investigations Unit where I was assigned the task of starting the Missing Persons and Vulnerable Persons Units (MPU and VPU). Maria was assigned there with me. Together, we investigated sexual assaults, domestics and even an attempted murder. Maria was always very good at interviewing victims, particularly females and children. She had natural skill and, despite her diminutive size, never appeared intimidated when dealing with suspects.

Two months later, I was transferred to the capital, Dili, and assigned to lead the National VPU. It was my job to draft policy and standard operating procedures for conducting investigations related to sex and gender-based offences. I created job descriptions and requirements for VPU investigators and served as a consultant for UN officials making new laws and legislation specifically addressing domestic violence.

One of the initiatives of the National VPU was to create training programs for the local police. We developed a three day training course for VPU investigators, funded by the Canadian International Development Agency. Our course was open to UN and East Timorese police alike, and I was excited to find that one of the course candidates was Maria. I had not seen her in a while, but was not surprised to learn that she had been permanently assigned to the investigations unit in Ermera District where she was helping to mentor new East Timorese police assigned there.

Maria's first day on the course was my last day in South East Asia. My time in East Timor had come to an end. I returned home to Canada a very different and, I hope, better Mountie than I had been when I had left. I'd learned a lot from the East Timorese and I hoped I had been able to pass on some of my knowledge to them. I hoped I had made that small contribution to the lives of just a few individuals, that positive impact at the personal level. And then there was Maria. She was a star student and a great police officer. I knew we'd never see each other again, but during the years following my mission, I often thought of her. I knew she was out there making a difference in her community.

Five years after leaving East Timor, I attended a UN sponsored conference in Brindisi, Italy. The conference was about gender-sensitive police reform in post conflict societies. There were delegates from around the world. I was there representing Canada. Guess who the delegate from East Timor was? You got it: none other than Maria. She had been promoted several times since I had seen her last and was now a Sub-Inspector (an equivalent rank somewhere between a staff sergeant and inspector in the RCMP). She technically outranked me!

Maria and I caught up on the last five plus years that had transpired in each other's lives. I was shocked to learn that several of her brothers who had been serving as members of the East Timor Police Service had been killed on duty during the riots in Dili that had occurred since I left East Timor. When she told me, it was with the eerily matter-of-fact demeanour I had come to realize often characterized people who had grown up under oppression and war. She didn't show much emotion. It was as if all the sadness had already been sucked out of her. Maria herself was now married.

Maria thanked me. She told me I had shown her what a female police officer can be and do, and said my example had helped her get where she was. Wow! I had always felt I had done some good in East Timor, but there it was: Affirmation at the personal level that I had indeed made a difference. And from someone who had obviously endured such challenges, it meant all the more to me

I carried the affirmation of Maria with me as I embarked on my second UN mission in 2011, this time to the Democratic Republic of the Congo where I monitored the building of police stations and personnel deployment in North Kivu province. One day, I attended the official inauguration of a newly constructed and equipped Police Nationale Congolaise commissariat in Masisi. I saw the hope on the faces of both the local villagers and the police officers sworn to serve them. It was overwhelming. Which of these police officers, newly trained in international approaches to policing, might be the next Maria, tirelessly working to build up their community from within?

The RCMP has given me the opportunity to work full-time in three Canadian provinces and make short-term trips to every corner of the country. I have also been grateful to have had the opportunity to work in numerous communities in two very different foreign countries. What have I learned? We all want the same things: We want our families to be safe and healthy; we want to be able to provide the basic necessities of life.

We want our communities to live in peace and security. We want to raise our children in a world that has a future. Protecting these values is why I became a police officer in the first place. The opportunity to mentor others as they pursue these goals within their own communities is what has made my time serving in UN missions so fulfilling.

HOPE COLLIDES
Constable April Dequanne

It's Wednesday, 7:00 a.m. and the sergeant calls the team in for a meeting. "We have a new lead on Jamal, but we need to move in quickly."

Jamal is a name that I recognize; we have been trying to locate him for weeks with little success. He is wanted on an immigration warrant for removal from Canada for serious criminal offences committed here.

"We have intel that he is armed and dangerous, and is only visiting his 'baby mom' over the next two days," the sergeant states. "And once we have visual, we'll get a warrant to gain access to the apartment and arrest him."

The sergeant goes on to explain that Jamal is six feet tall, 230 pounds, and has a lengthy criminal record, including drugs and weapons charges—we should be vigilant.

It's Tuesday, 3:00 p.m. and I've locked my guns and handcuffs away for the day and removed by soft body armour. They are replaced with a t-shirt that says "COACH" across the back. I am on my way to the Running and Reading Club at a middle school in Thistle Town, a tough neighbourhood in Toronto. Every Tuesday during the school year, I have the privilege of mentoring kids on how to achieve their goals through fitness and literacy. Our hope is to shorten the gap between the have and have-nots. It's a duty I feel just as strongly about as being a member of the RCMP. The kids have come to know me as "Coach April" and do not know that I am a police officer. Police and community relations are not at their best in Thistle Town, and I prefer the kids know me as Coach April rather than "Police Officer April."

Wednesday, 8:03 a.m., and I am sitting in my van in the parking lot of our target's apartment building. I see kids exiting the building by the dozen, some with parents, some without. Some with backpacks and lunch bags, some with none.

I think to myself, *No way would I let my child walk to and from school alone.*

Just last week there was a shooting in the community centre next to the school and a Crips versus Bloods gang war is raging. As kids file past my van, I slump low in my seat and give a silent prayer that I will not be seen. We are working uncomfortably close to my Running and Reading school.

Tuesday, 4:08 p.m.

"Coach April, can you help me tie my shoes?" asks Benjamin.

"Sure little buddy, then you can show me how fast you can run."

I bend over and tie up his shoes. Benjamin's shoes appeared far too big for his feet, and were well worn, with the soles beginning to peel off at the ends, but Benjamin still seems to float effortlessly across the gym floor with them securely tied on.

Wednesday, 8:18 a.m. and we are lined up outside the apartment door, weapons drawn, and ready to make our entry. We believe Jamal is inside the apartment along with the mother of his child and whoever else. We have been watching the apartment since our early arrival and there seems to be no movement inside and nobody has come or gone. We approach quietly. I can hear my heart pounding, and I can hear the quiet breaths of a teammate behind me. A teammate approaches the front door carrying the fifty pound metal door ram (what we affectionately call the "Master Key to the City"). Our Master Key is poised and ready for use.

Back to Tuesday, 4:36 p.m.

"When you're waiting for something good to happen to you."

That is the definition of "hope" given to us by one of our Running and Reading kids. Each week we introduce a new character-building word. The Running and Reading Club is not just about running and reading. It also provide a social development-rich environment so that when things get tough for kids, they have an arsenal of character attributes to draw from for personal protection and resilience.

Back to Wednesday, 8:23 a.m. Like slow motion, I see the door ram swing like a giant wrecking ball on a crane, the door shakes, the door frame cracks, and the deadbolt lock ricochets into the air. "Police!" The silence broken, I no longer hear the pounding of my heart or the breathing. We all made our presence known, and once inside the apartment we quickly realize that there are more people inside than our initial projections.

Tuesday, 4:42 p.m. and I'm reading from the book, *Terry Fox, A Story of Hope*. Sixty kids who have run out of energy are sitting quietly, hanging on every word I read. Sixty pairs of eyes and ears were looking to hear about "hope" from Coach April.

Wednesday, 8:24 a.m. We know who Jamal is and what threat he poses, but we don't know who the other three adults in the apartment are. Immediately the need to secure everyone is paramount to our safety. Unfortunately the individuals inside the apartment do not understand that need and the fight is on.

Tuesday, 4:44 p.m.

"Coach April, how come Terry never gave up?" a little voice from the back of the room enquires.

"Because Terry was very brave," I respond.

Wednesday, 8:25 a.m. and I've wrestled Jamal to the ground with a teammate positioned to put the handcuffs on him when I get a tap on the shoulder. I can hear my heart pounding, I can hear the breathing, and in slow motion, I turn not knowing the threat, ready to strike, and it is like I'm hit! A feeling of nausea fills my being; I shake my head as if the blinding would go away.

Tuesday, 4:58 p.m. Cleanup is done and we are preparing to send the kids on their way home.

"Remember to practice hope this week and be brave like Terry, because sometimes hope is found in the brave things we do."

The kids, tired from the hour of running, their minds filled with a story and hearts filled with hope, exit in a mad rush.

Wednesday 8:27 a.m.

"Coach April..."

I'm hit again, blind-sided, not with a fist or some inanimate object, but with a set of big brown eyes, filled with hope. I jump up and grab Benjamin to remove him from the living room, hoping to protect him from seeing what is about to happen to his father, Jamal.

Thursday 7:30 a.m. in the office boardroom—I am quiet during the debriefing of yesterday's arrest of Jamal. Gripped with the sorrow I feel for Benjamin, I don't have the energy to add to the conversation. Distracted, I sit silently with the hope that Benjamin understood that on Tuesday I was "Coach April" and Wednesday I was "Police Officer April" and on both days, I'm just trying to provide hope.

Be brave Benjamin, be brave!

LADY WITH THE ROSE
Corporal Veronica S.E. Fox

There is a belief among the members of the RCMP that the Force is a family. Some believe that we are all brothers and sisters, united together by the uniform, by our shared experiences and by the nature of our job. We laugh together and cry together, and when one of us falls in the line of duty, we each experience a personal sense of loss. We all do our part to remember those who have fallen and strive to hold them in our collective memory. One of the first ways we do this is at Depot during graduation week.

Graduation at Depot is a wonderful time. These are the days when the thirty-two members of a graduating troop join together one last time to celebrate before dispersing to the far reaches of Canada. A Depot graduation is a collection of many individual moments in time populated by proud parents and siblings, excited children, happy spouses and hopeful graduates. As the graduating members look back over their twenty-four weeks of training, there are many interactions punctuated with smiles, hugs, laughter and sometimes tears of joy. On graduation day, RCMP cadets are sworn in as constables before participating in the Sergeant Major's Parade for the last time. There is a dismounted cavalry drill routine, badge presentation ceremony and formal graduation banquet for the new members and their families. Before any of these other events, graduating Mounties also take time to remember important members of their new RCMP Family.

The day before graduation, the graduating troop and their families participate in an Ecumenical Chapel Service. When I graduated from Depot in January of 2006, our troop's service was held on a Sunday morning in the RCMP Chapel. The Chapel, which is located on the south side of the Depot Parade Square, is the oldest remaining building in Regina. Originally used in 1885 by the then North West Mounted Police (NWMP) as a guardhouse, it was later converted into a mess hall and canteen and finally a chapel in 1895. Although I had passed by the building many times during my training, Graduation Sunday was the first time I actually entered the chapel. When I did, I was immediately struck by how almost every feature of the building honoured the traditions of the RCMP. Large stained-glass memorial windows stood on each side of the altar. One depicted an RCMP constable in mourning and the other an RCMP trumpeter sounding reveille. Other smaller stained-glass windows in the chapel were dedicated to the RCMP members who gave their lives in World War II. The pews and alter were originals having been constructed over 100 years ago by NWMP carpenters. I marveled at the tradition, remembrance and reflections of family all around me. My troop mates and I were dressed in our red serge. We sat apart from our families, together as a troop. The service was serious and somber. This was a time for internal reflection.

After the service, our family and friends filed out of the chapel while my troop and I "formed up" and stood at attention on the parade square. Our troop's Right Marker called out commands and we marched along the west side of the parade square, halting at the cenotaph. Since 1934, names of fallen RCMP members have been recorded on the Depot Cenotaph. Each regular member, special constable and auxiliary constable whose name is etched in stone lost his or her life while acting in the line of duty. Since 1992, an annual service has been held at Depot to honour these fallen members. But in addition to this, graduating Mounties also remember in their own unique way. I'm not sure how or when this tradition began, but on the day before graduation, immediately following the chapel service, the graduating troop marches to the cenotaph, places a token of remembrance at its base, and offers salute. Civilian family members and friends observe from a short distance away, not interrupting this important moment as RCMP members remember their fallen brothers and sisters. In our troop, we selected a single member to place our token of remembrance. So on that very cold but clear Sunday morning in Regina, one of my troop mates broke ranks to place a single red rose at the base of the cenotaph. She stood for a moment, holding the rose in her hands as the troop looked on. After placing it, she offered a salute to the fallen before returning to our ranks. After a moment of silence, our Right Marker marched us off the parade square and to our waiting families.

Almost four years later, on a very different Sunday morning, approximately three hours south of Richmond, British Columbia where I was posted, four Lakewood, Washington police officers began their shift over coffee at a Pierce County coffee shop. The date was November 29, 2009. A single gunman entered the coffee shop and opened fire on the officers, killing them all. Two days later, the gunman was located by police. He was shot and killed while trying to escape arrest.

This was my first experience with such a tragic, large scale police death as a serving police officer. I honestly can't tell you where I was when I heard the news about the Lakewood police officers. I just remember thinking that I needed to do something both for the families of the four fallen officers and for their extended police family left behind. I clearly was not alone in this view. An official announcement was made regarding the upcoming public funeral for the Lakewood police officers, and all across the United States and Canada, individuals and groups began making plans to do what we police officers do in these situations: Show up and show support.

When it was clear that a significant number of Richmond Mounties were planning to attend the Lakewood Funeral, my detachment arranged for two minibuses (enough to transport about thirty serge-wearing Mounties) across the United States border. We all showed up to the detachment very early on the morning of the funeral. It was still dark out and it was cold. I was dressed in what I call "half-serge" which is breeches and high brown boots paired with a t-shirt or other civilian attire up top. Despite what you might see on television, it is unrealistic to submit oneself to a three hour bus ride wearing the scarlet tunic and Sam Browne belt. So on that morning, a troop of thirty or so Richmond Mounties wearing half-serge piled into two minibuses, neatly stowing thirty or so scarlet tunics, Sam Browne belts and Stetsons in the back. Our drivers (members from our own detachment who had volunteered to drive) took us to the highway and headed south.

At the border, a U.S. Customs Officer checked our passports. He specifically thanked us for our show of support. It was clear that everyone in law enforcement had been affected by the tragedy. Once in the United States, we made a quick stop to stretch our legs at a rest area just off the highway. Eyeing our breeches and high browns, a trucker asked us if we were part of some sort of riding club.

I smiled and said, "I guess you could say that."

When we hit the highway again heading south, it seemed to me that it was an average day in America. It was cold but fairly clear and people seemed to be going about their business as usual. Still, the American flags that I spotted here and there, flying at half-mast served to remind me of the somber reason for our visit. Recently, I had marched in a Canada Day parade. I had taken a bus packed with serge wearing Mounties to the venue. Almost to the point of cliché, on the way to our muster point, we sung *Oh Canada* and various fun folk songs. But this bus ride was very different. Everyone was somber and quiet. I pulled my toque down over my eyes and grabbed some sleep.

On the way in to Seattle, our minibuses got separated. Then, close to the Tacoma Dome, (the venue for the funeral), traffic snarled. It became apparent that there was absolutely nowhere to park. There were vehicles and people everywhere. The local firefighters had parked their fire trucks in pairs along the road; Large American flags flew overhead between their extended ladders. Police officers wearing many different uniforms clogged sidewalks and side streets and packed small businesses. We flagged down a random person who told us we had to park in a designated area several blocks away and then take a city shuttle bus to the venue. Our bus driver made the judgment call to "dump" all of our passengers so they could walk the short distance to the event location. He and I would then take our minibus to the designated parking area.

We parked our minibus illegally at the side of the road and 15 or so half-serge wearing Mounties piled out and began putting on the remainder of their dress uniform right there in the street. Many other police officers, all wearing their own unique ceremonial uniforms, walked past us as they converged on the Tacoma Dome. We exchanged nods but no words. It was like a strange sort of pilgrimage.

When our passengers were dressed and marching in twos towards the Tacoma Dome, the bus driver and I dropped the minibus at the designated parking area which turned out to be a very large warehouse. Inside, we parked bumper-to-bumper with other vehicles. There were police cars and other emergency vehicles from more jurisdictions than I could count. It was clear that once you parked, you weren't leaving until everyone else did. I wondered how we'd ever find our minibus again. After a short ride in the city shuttle bus, we joined the pilgrimage heading up the hill towards the Tacoma Dome.

They had set up port-a-potties along the road and my partner stopped to use one saying he would catch up with me, so I continued on alone. I passed a member of the local Emergency Response Team (often referred to in the American vernacular as SWAT). We made eye contact. Me, a five foot four female member dressed in the iconic red serge dress uniform of Canada's RCMP. He, a towering giant in black tactical gear, holding a very dangerous looking automatic firearm. We nodded to each other.

Thanks for showing up, he seemed to say.

Thanks for watching our backs, I wordlessly replied.

I looked up and saw some of this police officer's partners. Snipers dotted several nearby rooftops. Above them, police helicopters circled the area. Seeing the support from the members of the policing family who had stepped up to work so that the rest of us could grieve and show respect, I felt a new sense of pride and belonging.

I approached a hill behind which laid the open area where I'd heard all police were to "form up" before the ceremony. I felt a momentary sense of anxiety. How would I locate my group amongst all of the police officers gathering to enter the Tacoma Dome? But as I reached the crest of the hill, this concern melted away. A sea of red was spread out before me, as hundreds and hundreds of serge wearing Mounties stood in the massive parking lot. Clearly Richmond was not the only RCMP detachment that had sent members to the funeral. The parking lot was full of police officers from jurisdictions across Canada and the U.S. and yet I had no problem at all finding my group. I marched up and down the periphery of the sea of red until I found the other members from my minibus. Our driver found us soon after.

We heard rumours passed along from other Mounties closer to the entrance of the venue that the service had been delayed. This was because over 150 jurisdictions (many more than anticipated) had shown up to participate in the procession of police vehicles preceding the funeral. We passed the time by milling about, stamping our feet and blowing into our hands against the cold. Though it was sunny, it felt like the temperature had dipped below zero. Some members walked up and down the parking lot, looking for familiar faces. Some found troop mates or old coworkers that they had not seen in ages. Stories were shared as if no time had passed.

After some time, the group of a thousand or so Mounties decided to form up into ranks of four. I imagine this process must have been very interesting for the casual observer. How was it that over a thousand individuals were able to make a collective decision like this and execute it together without a designated individual leader coordinating the group? Actually, this was something that had been taught to us at Depot.

In drill we are taught that when on parade, every Mountie must look and move exactly as his or her neighbour. There must be an agreement in both appearance and action amongst everyone in the group. In this case, I imagine that someone within the group made a decision which was agreed upon and executed by his or her neighbours who then passed the message to those around them, who, in turn, continued the process. Like a stone making ripples in a pool of water.

I soon found myself standing in the middle of one of four very long ranks of Mounties. I was in the leftmost rank with three other ranks beside me to my right. We stood like this for some time waiting for another group decision to be made. A couple of self-appointed messengers marched up and down the outside ranks, announcing that we'd be entering the stadium soon. Somehow over a thousand Mounties came to attention. I later saw footage from the news helicopter that had been circling high overhead. We were one long line of red. One thousand Mounties in four ranks marched as one towards the Tacoma Dome. American news commentators called us their "friends from the North" and seemed to be at a loss for words when talking about our "impressive show of support." But to us, it wasn't about show. It was about being there for our extended police family, and acknowledging the loss and sacrifice of four officers from Lakewood.

As I marched in the ranks with my police family I focused on keeping in step and marching with precision as we had all been taught. My eyes were focused on the back of the head of the Mountie marching in front of me. I focused on the cadence of his step and ensured that my left heel hit the ground at the same time as his. After some time, I reached the end of the parking lot and marched across a small road where traffic had been blocked. Beyond this was the ramp leading to the stadium. A handful of observers stood there watching as we marched by. That is when I saw her. Out of the corner of my eye I saw a woman dressed all in black. She was standing to my left at the edge of the road. She was sobbing and stood there saying simply, "Thank you, thank you." She repeated her words over and over as row after row of Mounties marched past her. In her hands she held a single red rose. My breath caught in my throat and I choked back sudden tears as I was instantly thrown back to that moment years ago when my troop mate had placed a single red rose on the Depot Cenotaph.

The words of thanks from the lady at the Lakewood Funeral already meant so much, but the rose in her hands held special meaning. I have no idea who she was. A family member? A sister? A mother? A spouse? I doubt that she had any idea of the special significance that her rose tribute would have for a Mountie. As much as I wanted to, I could not stop to ask her name or find out who she was. I could not tell her what her simple gesture had meant to me. Instead, I marched onward along with the other Mounties into the Tacoma Dome.

The service let out several hours later in the early evening. It was already getting dark and it was now much colder than before. In the fading winter sunlight, my partners and I posed for photographs with police officers from many different departments. Most of the American police officers I met that evening had never seen a Mountie and many were eager to capture the moment before we departed for Canada. After this, we made our way back to our minibus and began our long journey home.

That night, amid the hubbub and activity, and on many occasions since then, I have found my mind drawn back to that significant moment at the Tacoma Dome and the lady with the rose.

ALL WORK, NO PAY
Auxiliary Constable Tammy Graham, Civilian Member

On November 12, 2004, thirty-nine year-old Auxiliary Constable Glen Evely went on a general duty ride-along in Vernon, British Columbia just as he had many times before. That same evening, while working as an RCMP Telecommunication Operator at the Southeast District Operational Communication Centre in Kelowna (OCC), I answered a call that remains forever etched in my memory.

Just after 2 a.m., a lady phoned in about a vehicle that was driving so erratically that she suspected the driver might be impaired. The caller was able to get close enough to the vehicle, which was still on the move, to read me the licence plate. Sometimes I regret having asked for that information, but that's my job. I ran the plate and determined that the vehicle (a black pickup truck) had recently been stolen from a neighbouring community. I sent an internal message to my dispatcher, a message that I knew would impact police response. As soon as the dispatcher broadcasted the details of the stolen vehicle, a number of police officers made it their mission to find it.

It was not long before two officers located the stolen pickup at a local gas station. They came close to apprehending the two suspects, but the pair was able to flee in the vehicle. Although the police officers backed off, the suspects continued speeding into the downtown core. There, the stolen pickup blew through a red light and slammed into a marked police cruiser that was legally crossing at an intersection. That police cruiser contained two members of the RCMP: A regular member who was driving, and Auxiliary Constable Glen Evely. Patrolling the city centre after bars close, Evely and his partner had been aware of the stolen vehicle but had not been actively attempting to locate it.

In the early morning hours of November 13, 2004, Auxiliary Constable Glen Evely died at the scene of the collision, leaving behind a wife and two young daughters. As was later reported by the media, Evely had been a former member of the Boy Scouts who had grown to become a husband, father, fisherman, ambulance driver, and forestry worker. He loved the outdoors and was devoted to his family. In 2002, Evely had become a sworn auxiliary constable and proudly served his community of Vernon for the next (and last) two years of his life.

Evely's death profoundly affected us all. OCC operators do not always have the chance to get to know the officers they dispatch for, but that does not make the feeling of losing one of our own any less horrible. That morning at the OCC, that terrible feeling set in. And it stayed. One challenge of being an OCC operator is lack of closure from hardly ever knowing how the incidents you dispatch police officers to end. But this time, the challenge was in knowing exactly how the file had ended. And still, closure never came.

Evely was not forgotten. Some of us attended a critical incident debriefing and many of Evely's colleagues shared memories and tributes during counselling sessions. Although the funeral was restricted to family, a massive public memorial was held in Vernon to allow the community a chance to mourn the loss of a local hero. Over 2000 police officers attended, as well as hundreds of emergency service workers and auxiliary constables. The RCMP Commissioner and Deputy Commissioner Bev Busson, who was Commanding Officer in E Division at the time, also came. During the memorial, Chaplain Jim Turner described Evely as a man who gave back more than he ever received.

Meanwhile, in hospital, it was still uncertain if Evely's police partner would survive. The constable had suffered serious brain injuries that left him in a coma for six weeks. When he did eventually wake up, it was to a life very different from before the crash. His twenty year career as a police officer was over and he had a long road of recovery before him. Over a year later, I met him for the first time during an RCMP hockey tournament in Vernon. He was our team's bench boss. Retired Constable Francois Grenier kissed the top of my head and told me he was sorry that I had had to be a part of that horrible incident. What? Me? No! I couldn't even fathom how his and many others' lives had been impacted. Humbled, I fought back tears as this fine gentleman stood before me. I have not seen him since that tournament but I still remember his words.

Long after the memorial, when we had all done our best to settle back into the routine of work, Evely's killer was sentenced. He admitted to having stolen the pickup and to having driven it dangerously. He said he had been high on cocaine at the time. I was not called to attend court but I did receive word of the outcome by email. That is how I learned he had been convicted of criminal negligence causing bodily harm and death and that he'd been handed a sentence of seven years in prison. I do not know where he is now, and I actually do not much care.

Meanwhile, Auxiliary Constable Glen Evely is not only remembered, he is honoured. Annie Lavigne, his wife, was presented with the RCMP Memorial Memento in 2012, an award recognizing police officers who have sacrificed their lives while serving their communities. As with other auxiliary constables who have passed away on duty under similar circumstances, including Frederick Abel, Joseph Balmer, and Dennis Fraser, the memory of Auxiliary Constable Glen Evely lives on.

Evely's death was one of the factors that inspired me to become an auxiliary constable. His story stuck with me. His tragedy made me want to do good things for my community. So, in October 2008, I was sworn in as an auxiliary constable in Nanaimo, joining the ranks of the more than 2,000 members who had served in the role in British Columbia since the program commenced in 1963.

Auxiliary constables are sworn, provincial, uniformed peace officers who receive relevant training allowing them to work closely with members of the RCMP in matters related to crime prevention and community policing. When I signed up, I agreed to meet the minimum annual commitment of 160 volunteer hours and was excited to explore the options available to me on which I could spend that time. For the most part, auxiliary constables are able to devote their volunteer hours to various programs as they see fit, catering to their own interests as long as they fall within the confines of the program.

In December 2008, shortly after I began the program, I jotted down my initial thoughts and goals:

> *I chose to enroll in the Auxxiliary Program so that I could serve my community and better understand it and the individuals within it. In a short time, I have discovered that I am enjoying the Auxiliary Program far beyond my expectations. I only hope I can give back as much as I am receiving. I am amazed at the amount of experience in the program and the willingness of those involved to share their knowledge. Every*

shift that I complete, I am in awe of someone or something. Ultimately, my goal is to continue on the same path that I've started, gleaning as much as I can from different RCMP sections and contributing as much and in as many ways as I can within the program's parameters.

Several years later, I am still continually striving to attain my goal in this area and doing so has been one of my most rewarding undertakings. I see being an auxiliary constable as both an honour and an opportunity to learn about myself and my community.

As I learned in the Auxiliary Program, there is room for everyone in the world of volunteering and there are countless ways to serve the community. During our monthly meetings, we would learn about upcoming events and safety initiatives that we could assist with. At first, I signed up for anything and everything: Career fairs, safety talks, specialized training held by members or partner agencies, school visits, local fairs, a local hockey team's appreciation day, marine-related orientations, and the list went on. Then I branched out on my own, setting up shifts with specific sections in the RCMP including First Nations Community Policing, Forensic Identification Services, School Liaison, and General Duty. I even helped lay down a training track for the Police Dog Section. I cannot even begin to express how thankful I am for all the regular members who were so receptive to sharing their expertise while I accompanied them.

Although I thoroughly enjoyed getting a taste of as many great programs as I could, as time went on, I began focusing on the initiatives that inspired me the most. I discovered a passion for First Nations Community Policing and working with youth, and from that point forward, I devoted most of my volunteer hours to these areas.

Having previously been both a youth group volunteer and sports coach, I believe that children and teens are tremendously impressionable and that their early experiences mould and shape the rest of their lives. That's why I believe being a positive force in the lives of youths is one of my most important responsibilities as an auxiliary constable.

Many youth never get the chance to meet a peace officer. Others sometimes meet police under unfortunate circumstances. My presence in elementary and secondary school classrooms allows young people to ask questions, hear about safety issues relevant to their age, and maybe learn that a person in uniform isn't a bad thing. I believe that if I can help just one youth see the police as a positive element in their community, perhaps that child or teen will grow into an adult who is supportive of the police and contributes to society.

I teach secondary students about the dangers of drinking and driving and how to be safe at parties and in relationships. For the elementary students, the topics are a bit more basic. Retro Bill is a tall-haired zany guy whose videos help me teach young kids about self-esteem and safety. His crazy antics and hilarious voice are a favourite with many of the kids, but I appreciate his ability to reach the children at their level, driving home real world lessons about making safe and healthy life choices.

In January of 2013, I became a proud Drug Abuse Resistance Education (D.A.R.E.) instructor. D.A.R.E. is a well-known safety and decision-making awareness program taught in countless schools in North America. The curriculum teaches children in Grades Five and Six the social skills necessary to make healthy decisions around drugs, alcohol, and other aspects of life. One of the great things about D.A.R.E. is that it is taught by uniformed peace officers. Every time I suit up in my uniform to visit the classroom, I feel a sense of pride that I am able to represent the RCMP and help develop young children. My role as a D.A.R.E. instructor has taken me as far as Iqaluit, Nunavut, where I taught the D.A.R.E. program to several classes at a local middle school during a short-term transfer for work. It was such a rewarding experience, and I continue to teach now that I am back in Nanaimo.

Serving as an auxiliary constable has also allowed me to explore my interest in First Nations Community Policing. Over the past few years, in addition to the training offered through the RCMP, I have attended several Indigenous awareness conferences and workshops on both my own time and dime. It has been worth it. I have greatly benefited and grown from the abundance of local, national, and international knowledge. I continue to apply my learning by building relationships with various First Nations communities on Vancouver Island and have been privy to sacred ceremonies because of this personal approach. I am also the First Nations Liaison at OCC in Nanaimo where I created a comprehensive resource binder and narrated PowerPoint about the communities we serve. I have volunteered at the Coast Salish Games and participated in a fishing program for First Nations youths, but my most memorable experiences are by far the Indigenous canoe journeys.

Every summer since 2009, I have participated in Tribal Journeys, an annual journey wherein Pacific Northwest nations and tribes paddle the "ancient highways of the ancestors" for several days in ocean-going canoes to a pre-determined destination in Canada or the United States. During the trips, canoe families camp on the lands of various nations and tribes along the way. At each stop there is a feast, followed by the sharing of stories and partaking in traditional festivities and ceremonial protocols. The whole journey culminates in a large protocol with thousands of people at the final destination.

Indigenous canoe journeys are significant cultural events wherein those who take part are able to connect with their culture, learn the principles for healthy living and observe ancestral traditions and protocols. These journeys are also valuable relationship building events that connect community organizations and Indigenous nations. The RCMP has long recognized the value of such programs and takes turns with other agencies hosting a one-week journey called Pulling Together, which is held in a different British Columbia community each summer. I've grown a lot from my participation in both Tribal Journeys and Pulling Together.

During the 2010 Tribal Journey, I paddled for ten days as a member of the Kw'umut Lelum canoe family to Washington State. Kw'umut Lelum Child and Family Services is an agency that oversees the welfare of several Indigenous youths living within nine Vancouver Island Coast Salish communities.

Participating in the journey was both exhilarating and exhausting. The sights were amazing, but the beauty of the coastline paled in comparison to the transformation I witnessed in the young participants. Everyone was spiritually nourished by the songs, dances, traditions, hard paddling and forging of interpersonal relationships. I recall one youth in particular who expressed her strong dislike for police at the beginning of the journey. By the time we got to the States, she and the police officer in our canoe family had formed such a strong bond that she asked her to help wash her hair in the sink of a home near our campsite. For me, that moment confirmed the potential of immersive experiences like canoe journeys and the benefit to peace officers engaging with the communities they police.

To this day, I am grateful to be a part of the Kw'umut Lelum canoe family, an invitation that came as a direct result of my being an auxiliary constable. My canoe family permitted me to document our 2010 journey, which included participants from various tribes and nations sharing with me the history and traditions behind it. The final result of this openness was my master's thesis: *A Tribal Journey: Canoes, Traditions, and Cultural Continuity.* I was proud to be able to explore the positive cultural and communicative impact of canoe journeys on youth, particularly the ones I travelled with. The journey was a self-defining experience for many of them and also for me.

Being an RCMP auxiliary constable has allowed me to serve my community and develop myself on a personal level, and I didn't have to become a regular member to do so. It has truly been a win-win experience. In the end, it does not matter if you are a teacher, businessman, secretary, welder, saleswoman, doctor, construction worker, or accountant. Anyone permitted to volunteer with the RCMP can apply in communities that have active Auxiliary Programs. Serving my community, I often think about these words:

> *Everybody can be great because anybody can serve. You don't have to have a college degree to serve. You don't have to make your subject and your verb agree to serve. You only need a heart full of grace, a soul generated by love.*
>
> *– Martin Luther King Jr.*

Although being an auxiliary constable is literally "all work and no pay," it does not actually feel like work, and the payment is immeasurable. The reality is auxiliary constables do what we love and love what we do.

PRIDE IN UNIFORM
Sergeant Penny Hermann

I really enjoyed the Drill Program when I went through training at Depot in 1996. My troop and I spent countless hours marching around the training facility's drill hall as cadets. Fourteen years later, I stepped back into the familiar Depot drill hall, this time as a drill instructor.

In the three and a half decades since women first joined the RCMP, there have only been six female drill instructors at Depot, including me. At the time, I was the only woman working in a unit dominated by men. Historically, men have typically been drill instructors.

Drill has always been an integral part of RCMP training. But what is the point of it? To break it down, drill is the orderly movement of a group of people. Historically, armies have used drill to appear more imposing to an enemy. By moving with precision in unison, the group looks more formidable and organized regardless of its size. The RCMP uses drill not to instill fear, but to endow cadets with a sense of organizational belonging, self-discipline and teamwork. Every Mountie receives the same training, learning to pay attention to detail, follow direct orders and, most importantly, remain calm and focused in times of chaos. Having said that, when you think *drill instructor*, what comes to mind? There are plenty of movies out there that offer a suggestion: typically a drill instructor is male, loud, in-your-face, quick on the draw usually with insulting one-liners and always very intimidating.

Now to tell you a little bit about myself: When I went through Depot as a cadet, I was naive and not very confident. Of course, years on the road had helped with that, but at 5'4-", how could I ever be considered "intimidating?" I knew I had what it took to be a police officer, but did I really have the extra that it would take to be a good drill instructor?

It just so happened that my old drill corporal was now the Sergeant Major and my supervisor. He and the other members in the drill unit were very supportive and encouraging. I told them that my biggest fear was those one-liners. RCMP drill instructors do not deliver insults like you've perhaps seen in the movies. Our one-liners are meant to make light of mistakes rather than humiliate. Success is when an entire troop fights to maintain composure despite the laughter welling up inside. I knew that I had a good sense of humour, but I was not too sure that I would be able to quickly come up with good lines on the fly.

One thing I was not worried about was being able to make myself heard. I credit my large booming voice to having worked as a lifeguard at a wave pool for so many years.

I don't know how many times people came up to me and said, "That was *you*?"

They'd often follow up this question with, "But you're so tiny!"

Despite the support of my unit and my own trust in my abilities, I was very nervous the first time I had to lead "hour one on the floor." This is the first time a troop of cadets is on the drill floor for class. I had to memorize the lesson plan, ensure I did not run out of time, be prepared to pick out mistakes that the cadets were making and also set the "presence" and tone by being in the cadets' faces. My coworkers assisted me when necessary and I pulled off a respectable first "hour one on the floor." None of the cadets were any the wiser that it had been my "hour one" just as much as it had been theirs.

I became a drill instructor that grown men feared. When inspecting a troop at the beginning of class, it was interesting to see men literally shaking. Sometimes sweat would drip from their hands. I found it humorous that I would make people shake. I am not an in-your-face kind of person, but I knew that I had a role to play. The truth is, there are people out there in the real world who do not like police officers. My cadets had to learn how to remain professional at all times, even if someone was "in their face." It was my job to teach them how.

Working in the Drill Unit was a transformative experience. I had gone from teaching Applied Police Sciences in a classroom where my cadets told me that they could never see me as a drill instructor, to leading troops of cadets who said that they could not imagine me instructing in a classroom. I had replaced my naïveté with confidence. My troop mates could not believe the unassuming cadet they had graduated with was the leader I had become. I had changed, for the better. I had a good reputation of being firm but fair, and was proud of it.

One day, I invited my husband (who is not a member of the RCMP) to watch one of my "hour ones" at the drill hall. I should emphasize the fact that my family, including my spouse, had never before heard me yell. By the end of the session, my husband had a stress headache and a stiff neck that lasted several hours. He was not used to seeing me in such a role and was very appreciative that I was not like that at home.

It was tradition that each graduating troop performed a marching routine of dismounted cavalry drill called a *pass-out*. The drill instructor was responsible for choreographing the routine, and the troop worked to the best of their ability to deliver it with precision. When it came to drill, I was an unashamed perfectionist and I was firm that my pass-out routines meet a high standard. As a result, I would spend my own time at Depot during evenings and weekends, working with my troop to get them ready for their big day. My family was always supportive and understanding. They even came to see many of my troops perform the pass-outs that I had choreographed.

My family has always been my primary support and this has extended to include my role as a drill instructor. I am a mother and a wife; I have two children that are heavily involved in many activities. I balanced my family and work commitments with my own involvement as a national synchronized swimming judge. Throughout my career, my husband has been particularly supportive. He was always there to step in to help with the kids and household needs while working full time. His support did not change when I went to the Drill Unit which had added time commitments in the form of early morning parades which start at 6:30 a.m., the Sunset Parade (a City of Regina tourist attraction), graduations and various other ceremonial duties.

The duties of a police officer extend beyond the average nine to five work day of the mainstream workforce. For a drill instructor, there is even more to deal with. It is our responsibility to teach the history of the Force and instill pride in the uniform amongst other things previously mentioned. It is a responsibility that I am passionate enough about to write several more pages on this alone. I would, however, like to end my time with you by telling you about one of the highlights of my career which happened while I was working in the Drill Unit.

I always said that if I helped just one person in my career, that was all that mattered. I never really considered that doing so in my role as a drill instructor would have such a profound impact on my own life.

It was September 2012, and I volunteered to put a project together for the Commissioner. The idea was a simple one: create a card for every fallen member on our cenotaph. The card was to be no ordinary card. It had to be something special. In fact, it was hoped that it would be something that each cadet would carry with them throughout their career. A draft template was created. The card was to be folded along two seams. When it was opened, on the left side would be a copy of the Honour Roll in calligraphy. In the centre of the card would be the name of a fallen member along with his or her picture (if I could obtain it). Finally, on the right side would be a simple narrative describing the hobbies, interests or other features that made this person unique.

I decided to start with a person that I had worked with in the field: Cpl. Jim Galloway, an accomplished dog handler who was shot and killed when assisting the Edmonton Emergency Response Team in Spruce Grove, Alberta in 2004. I had no idea of how tough this was going to be. Jim had assisted on some of my files when I was posted in Morinville, Alberta. So many memories went through my head. I cried. When I did the research for the narrative, I cried some more. I did not want to fail to do justice to his memory and the sacrifice that he had made.

After Jim's card was done, I went to the top of the list: Honour Roll Number 1 — Sub. Cst. John Nash. The information available about many fallen members was very limited. I did library and online research and even went to the National Archives in Ottawa. At the time, there were 231 names on the cenotaph. I made sure a card was made for each and every one. While doing my research, I often found myself thinking about each fallen member's family. Had they been able to move on after such a tragic loss? How were they doing now? At times I found myself in tears reading the stories of how our fallen members had passed. I started to look at life a bit differently. I made more of an effort to appreciate the time I had with my own family.

Often, I would dig up information that led me to relatives or descendants of the fallen. Initially, I found it difficult making contact with the relatives and loved ones. How are you supposed to start a conversation like that over the phone or by email? They did not know me, nor I them. Why would they want to discuss such personal matters with a stranger? Would I be opening up old wounds? Were they angry or bitter towards the Force? Would they be angry with me for contacting them?

Still, I was excited about this program. The RCMP was taking the initiative to remember our fallen members in a unique, important and meaningful way. I was eager to share this with these families. I wanted to let them know that we remembered and cared too. I also wanted these cards to be as accurate as possible and having a loved one look over what I had written gave it that authenticity I wanted and made it more personal. It also gave a chance for family members to open up and share stories that I had otherwise never have known.

The program has had such a significant impact which I believe has surpassed what anyone had expected, especially me. I have heard from cadets who have gone the extra mile and done further research on their "silent partner," making their own connections with family members. I have spoken with loved ones of some fallen who have told me that this project opened lines of communication between estranged family members. Many family members want to know who will be carrying their loved one with them out on patrol. Although I cannot give out cadet names, I do encourage those receiving the cards to do their own research and make contact with the family when possible. Many of the family members are comforted by the thought that their loved one will truly never be forgotten.

The Silent Partner Program reinforced in my mind the concept that our fallen members were more than police officers; they were normal people doing an extraordinary job. Having heard their stories has made them that much more human for me. I no longer think in terms of Honour Roll numbers carved into a stone cenotaph. I think of fathers, mothers, brothers, sisters, sons, daughters, spouses ... Memorial Parades mean even more to me now. We march because they cannot. What started as me wanting to help someone, ended up as them helping me. For that I will always be grateful.

PART III

NOWHERE NEAR ORDINARY

BOATING 101
Constable Christy Veenstra

At around midnight on one particularly cold and rainy night, while working general duty in North Vancouver, British Columbia, my partner and I were dispatched to investigate an uncompleted call to 9-1-1. There wasn't any information available. All we knew was that a female had called police asking for help and that our call-taker had heard shouting in the background before the line disconnected.

The call had come from a residence up on Indian River Drive, a road to the extreme east of the city. There were very few houses on this road as it was difficult to access. As my partner and I drove down the road, we soon realized it ended at the 5500 block, which was a significantly lower address than the one we had been dispatched to. Back then, we had no cellular mapping programs, no computers in our cars and no smart phones. To get around, we relied on these things called "map books." When we could not locate the address using this, we headed to a nearby marina to see if we could get some insight.

My partner and I parked our car and walked around, asking the locals if they knew a route to our destination. Some people were truly unable to help us while others simply did not want to. Someone finally told us that the only way to our intended destination was by boat. So what to do? Some people would call a friend. In our case, we called our sergeant for advice. I recall his words exactly: "Do whatever you think is necessary."

And that is exactly what we did. I considered the circumstances—we were dispatched to a high priority file where someone's life could be in danger. We really had no idea of what was going on at the residence and could not confirm anyone's safety until we got there. There was apparently no way to get to the residence by police car and if we called the Coast Guard, or any other available marine assistance, they would have to pick us up before heading to the scene. There was nothing left to do but improvise. I decided that we needed a boat, and we needed it right away.

My partner and I split up and canvased the marina, looking for a boat to hire for our cruise up Indian Arm. Suddenly, barely anyone seemed to be awake and, oddly, the few who were, did not appear to have any interest in chartering their vessels to us for official police business. But finally, my partner found a volunteer. Well, sort of...

Joe, as we will call him, offered to lend us his boat, but after talking to him I knew there was no way he could captain it for us. It seemed to me that Joe had consumed a few too many "wobbly pops" that evening. Standing on the dock, Joe smiled at me, swaying back and forth as if already out at sea. In good conscience I couldn't let him man the helm or even join us on the journey. Still, he was offering us his boat.

Joe asked where we were heading and we gave him the address. He scoffed and told us that our land address was useless to him. He needed the nautical coordinates. My partner and I looked at each other and then sheepishly admitted that we did not have any nautical coordinates. Quite frankly, I did not even really know what nautical coordinates were. We were, however, confident that we would be able to find the place we were looking for once we got to the general area. At least, this is what we told Joe. Anyway, how many people could be up in that area at this time of night? I figured we would just look for lights or something. To be honest, at that point I would have said anything necessary to get Joe to help us out. It was cold and miserable out and I wanted to get up the Indian Arm as soon as possible to ensure everyone was safe so that my partner and I could find our way back to our warm police car.

Joe eyed us. I suppose he was weighing his options just as I had done earlier. Finally, he agreed to help us. I had no intention of letting Joe drive a boat, so I took the lead. But my partner and I were just about to step onto what we assumed was Joe's nice, safe looking yacht, when he informed us that *Big Money* was not his vessel. Joe, swaying slightly, pointed down the pier towards the boat he meant to lend us.

I could feel my heart drop into my patrol boots. Joe's boat appeared to be little more than a tin can. It didn't even have a cabin. A closer inspection revealed that it was basically a metal rowboat with a motor attached. I was fairly confident that Joe had attached the motor himself, probably while indulging in some of those "wobbly pops." I wondered what MacGyver would have thought of the work.

Joe's boat was rusty. She looked to be as old as the *St. Roch*, the famous RCMP Arctic patrol vessel which began her career in 1928. That evening, I decided that I was looking at the *St. Roch II*. She had probably been launched shortly after her predecessor's retirement.

Despite my apprehension, duty called. We needed to help someone in need, so the *St. Roch II*, whatever her condition, would have to do. We asked Joe about life jackets. He rummaged around in the hull and handed over two museum pieces that appeared as if they'd been stolen from a *Titanic* exhibition. I suspected that these "life jackets" would be effective only in helping us get to the bottom of the ocean faster, but we had nothing else, so on they went.

Into the *St. Roch II* my partner and I went, and after a quick lesson from Joe on how to start and steer the vessel, we were off. Joe stayed behind, swaying and waving to us from the pier as we headed out into the night.

My partner steered the boat. As he was junior to me in service, he got to endure being called "Gilligan" for the duration of the cruise. I, of course, was "the Captain." As captain, I took my rightful place at the bow (front) of the boat. My self-appointed job was to make sure we didn't hit anything. I believe that's referred to as "navigating" in nautical parlance.

As we left the marina, I quickly realized how dark it can be out on the water in the middle of the night along Indian Arm. It was pitch black and we were heading into the middle of who-knows-where with no boating experience, no lights and not even an intoxicated Joe to guide us. Since Joe had MacGyvered the engine of *St. Roch II*, I figured I could MacGyver a solution of my own. My trusty police flashlight became the boat light. I lay down in the bow of the boat and shone my flashlight forward towards the water so that Gilligan could see where we were going. Off we went to save the person in distress.

Gilligan and I were on the water for only a few minutes when I realized just how cold it can get when you're on the water. I tried to duck down in the boat to stay out of the wind, but even with this, my hands and face soon felt numb with cold. We made our way up the Indian Arm, maneuvering around several logs. In the distance we could see what looked like a light beacon. We decided to head towards it. The beacon led us to a nice big dock with plenty of space for Gilligan to maneuver. I noticed a nice 50 foot yacht moored nearby.

All I could think was, *Don't hit it. Don't hit it.*

While coming in to dock, we were again reminded that we had no idea of what we were doing. I grabbed for the dock while instructing Gilligan to cut the engine thinking we would drift in slowly. Instead, Gilligan accidentally jolted the engine and we jerked forward causing me to crush my arm between the dock and the *St. Roch II*. I had a few choice words to say about that while Gilligan continued attempting to dock.

While we were still sorting ourselves out, our 9-1-1 caller made her way down to the dock. She was quite amused by our attempts at docking. Finally, we managed to get the *St. Roch II* settled into place and climbed onto the dock feeling reasonably pleased with ourselves.

We dealt with our complainant's issue. No fight, no arrests, not even a real emergency. Typical. Still, we had responded to a call for assistance against all odds. We'd made sure our complainant was okay and had made her feel valued. I guess it was worth the trip.

After concluding our investigation, we headed back out to the *St. Roch II* and pointed our vessel down Indian Arm. Eager to return to the marina and our police vehicle, Gilligan and I decided to kick it up a notch. The engine of the *St. Roch II* revved, and Gilligan and I prepared for full speed ahead. Instead, the engine sputtered and then died completely. Gilligan tried his best to restart the engine but it was to no avail. We decided to paddle. It was at this point that we learned that there was only one oar aboard the *St. Roch II* and that it wasn't exactly in prime condition. I think that a tennis racket would probably have served us better. I wondered if it was now time to call the Coast Guard. But, how embarrassing would that be? Maybe if we sat drifting for long enough, someone would notice that we'd been away for a little too long and would send help with no humiliating radio calls for assistance required from us. Or maybe we would eventually just drift south to the marina.

After what seemed like an eternity, Gilligan was able to start the engine! With his precision piloting and my excellent direction as captain, we were able to make our way down the Indian Arm and back to the safety of the marina. Joe was sure pleased to have the *St. Roch II* back and we were pleased to take our leave of her and be back on dry land.

After that evening, our sergeant never again gave us permission to do "whatever we thought was necessary." Apparently, he had meant for us to wait for the Coast Guard, not commandeer a boat. Maybe he should have been more specific.

CORTEZ
Staff Sergeant Nav Hothi

I t was shaping up to be a very hectic day in the Forensic Identification Section. Early into my shift, I had been notified of a homicide and was awaiting word about the search warrant. A body had been found in the driveway of a residence and investigators were drafting documents to get permission from the courts to have full access to the property. I tried to get as much paperwork and organizing done as possible while waiting for the warrant. I knew it would not arrive until late in my shift, so I made the best use of the time that I had.

It was not until late afternoon when the investigators finally arrived at the office, signed search warrant in hand. Showtime. My partner and I packed our van with all the equipment we knew we would need, and lots more we probably would not, before heading to scene.

I parked at the front of the house. Climbing out of my van, I nodded to the young constable in uniform doing scene security. I adjusted my duty belt. I wore a modified version of the typical RCMP uniform which included dark blue fatigues bearing the RCMP crest, thick soled black boots and, of course, the duty belt. In case you didn't know: real-life forensic work is nothing like on TV. No stilettos and flowing hair here.

Ducking under a line of yellow police tape at the edge of the property, I immediately noticed a body, wrapped in clear plastic, lying on the driveway. It was a deceased male. Nearby, a pickup truck sat, its back gate down. Whose truck was that? Had someone tried to put the body in the truck bed? Who was the deceased? How did he die? And where? All questions that needed answers, and it was my job to find them.

I walked into the house in hopes of finding the evidence I needed to solve the crime. The place had already been cleared by uniformed police officers first called to scene and a second time, more methodically, as soon as the warrant had been approved. I walked around confidently from room to room, getting an overview of the entire scene before processing it.

In the living room, I found a pool of blood and a gun casing. Hmm ... this was what they called "a clue." A quick walk through of the rest of the house, and I located a possible murder weapon along with a roll of plastic likely to match the wrapping around the body. Lots of questions answered in record time. This was shaping up to be a pretty cut-and-dry file.

My partner and I divided up the tasks: he began taking photographs of the scene outside the house while I began videotaping the scene inside. I kicked all other police officers out of the house. I did not want any voices or conversations to be recorded on the video and I didn't want any police officers seen in the frames as this would take away from the overall view of each room. Unlike the film industry, everything we shoot, we keep. Every shot, good or bad is handed over to crown counsel as evidence. There is no picking and choosing the best shot and no editing room floor.

The videotaping process was fairly simple and very methodical. I started at the front of the house, capturing the deceased on the driveway, and moved inside. It was all rather routine, until I got to the living room. This was the room where the homicide itself had likely occurred. I set up my camera in one corner to get a view of the stairs and hallway leading from the room. In my head, I had already planned a number of different shots. I turned on the video camera.

"Fuck you," said a man's voice. It was quiet, but it was crystal clear.

I had never heard my partner or the two investigators I knew at scene use such language before. I was puzzled. Perhaps it was that constable I'd seen doing scene security. Either way, my shot was ruined, and I was angry. Flicking off the camera, I stomped down the stairs and found everyone outside.

"Who was just swearing?" I demanded.

"Wasn't us. We were outside."

"You weren't inside just now?" I asked. "Because someone said 'fuck you' as clear as day when I was inside."

The three looked at each other as if I'd finally lost my marbles.

"Wasn't us," they said.

I spun on my heel and stomped back into the house. Grumpily, I returned to the living room and turned on my video camera and began recording again.

"Fuck you."

I looked out the living room window. There were my partner and the two investigators standing on the street at the end of the driveway. Then that uniformed scene security constable came into view, joining the group and passing out bottles of water. My blood turned to ice. There was someone in the house with me!

I drew my gun and turned to search the kitchen and bedrooms, where I'd thought the voice had come from.

"Fuck you."

Now it seemed to be coming from the living room!

I'd heard stories from veteran members in forensics. They'd reported strange occurrences at crime scenes. Things that were not easily explained. Some even claimed that sometimes the deceased hangs around for a while. I personally hadn't fully made up my own mind about such things, but what if there was some credence to those stories?

"Fuck you."

It was right behind me. I whirled around and said in a low, deep voice, "Police, show your hands."

No answer.

I started to look behind every piece of furniture and under every couch. You'd be surprised where some people can hide. While looking under one couch I heard it again, to my right. My head snapped around and I focused on a shadowy corner of the room.

Something was tucked in behind a curtain. Was there someone hiding there? Getting closer, I saw a bed sheet draped over something large. I walked up and yanked the sheet, gun still drawn.

A beautiful large, red macaw stared back at me from behind the wire bars of his cage. It had rainbow feathers of red, blue and green. The macaw tipped its head and blinked a few times. I could see its pupil dilate as it stared at me. It puffed its chest and spoke.

"Fuck you," he said.

I sighed with relief and made a mental note to apologize to the members outside for being so curt with them earlier.

Well, I'd located a possible eye-witness to the events in the living room so I did what cops do.

"So who did this?" I asked.

No answer.

I asked again. This time, I got a reply.

"Cortez! Cortez!"

I dutifully wrote this down in my notebook. I asked a few more questions but the macaw's vocabulary was clearly limited to what I'd already heard so I continued with the video, ensuring I had a great shot of the bird in case anyone later doubted my account of events.

Many hours later, my partner and I finished processing the crime scene and a few weeks after that, I officially wrapped up my portion of the investigation. My findings were documented and shared with investigators; my file was concluded and I thought no more about it. I got on with the other files and investigations that needed my attention.

About a year later, it was time for court. A suspect had been charged and trial date had been scheduled. I set about disclosing all my materials and evidence to both crown and defense counsel. My submissions included that video tape. I warned crown that the tape may not be suitable for court proceedings and we debated playing it without audio. But viewing a video with no audio is actually not easy for people to do. Normal background noises like leaves rustling in the breeze or creaking floorboards in a house actually give the viewer some context for what they are watching. As this was a jury trial, it was important that evidence be easily interpretable to the average person, so we kept the audio.

I was oddly anxious on trial date. Do not get me wrong, I love attending court. I love explaining the nuances of forensic processes and investigation, I love sharing my findings specific to each case. I even love being cross-examined by defence. I especially love a jury trial. So often, it appears on the surface that counsel, and even judges, find my evidence boring or routine. They listen to me talk and ask questions, all without ever giving any indication as to what they are thinking. I guess this makes sense, they're used to the courtroom and the presentation of evidence. But to jurors, things are new and sometimes exciting. They seem to hang on your every word and react to what they hear through body language and facial expression. But instead of being eager to present my evidence, I felt an uncommon sense of nervousness. Court is a formal affair. There are official titles and rules of decorum. No one swears. I was prepped and ready to go, and my evidence was extensive. Still, I was worried that the macaw's foul language might be a distraction in the courtroom or offend a spectator in the galley or a juror in the box or, worse yet, the judge.

In the courtroom, I took the stand. After officially stating my name and rank and promising before the court that my testimony would be true, I pushed play on the video. The courtroom was equipped with a large television screen which allowed the judge, jury and gallery, packed with spectators, to view the video I'd shot that day. Everyone watched in silence.

The screen faded up to a shot of the end of a driveway with a house visible in the background. The camera panned and a body, wrapped in clear plastic, came into view. The deceased was a male lying on the driveway near a pickup truck which was parked with its back gate down. Exactly as I remembered. I watched in silence as the video progressed. The camera proceeded up the driveway and into the home in one continuous shot. Inside the residence, the scene changed to the living room. I watched the face of the presiding judge in my peripheral vision. I knew what was to come.

And there it was. The judge frowned, and the jurors tipped their heads, much like that macaw had done. And there it was again. The second time, the judge interrupted.

"Corporal," he said, "whose voice is that on the video?"

I hit the pause button.

"My Lord, it is a parrot," I replied.

"A parrot?" he asked with some incredulity.

"Yes, my Lord," I said.

"Alright, Corporal," said the judge almost suspiciously. "Proceed,"

The video continued. At every instance of the foul phrase there came an audible twitter from the spectators and jury. Meanwhile, the frown on the forehead of the judge deepened. I wanted to crawl under the witness box. I was sure to be chastised by the presiding judge.

After what seemed like an eternity, the parrot came into clear view on the video. He sat there in his cage, looking regal in beautiful bright red, blue and green feathers. After a moment, he puffed out his chest and tipped his head, looking directly at the camera.

"Fuck you, Cortez," he said.

A roar of laughter erupted from the spectator gallery, accompanied by a twitter of giggles from the jury. The judge did a face-palm. And I wanted to disappear.

As the video progressed to show the rest of the house, the courtroom quietened down. The next three hours of my testimony went much more smoothly and cross-examination by defence was thorough but painless. My initial unease disappeared, replaced by confidence knowing that I had done my job thoroughly and professionally despite the presence of a profanity spewing feathered friend. The accused pled guilty before crown even rested their case. We never did figure out who "Cortez" was.

DUCK AND COVER
Corporal Veronica S.E. Fox

It was another beautiful day in Richmond, British Columbia. The sun was out and big puffy white clouds drifted lazily across the blue sky. I climbed back into my police car after attending to a routine call in the business district and began writing up my report, keeping half an ear on the radio.

One of my corporals was dispatched to a call for assistance at a residence south of my location. A constable was sent to a shoplifting not far from where I was. Someone else advised dispatch they would be off radio for a bit at the office for follow-ups. It was definitely a routine sort of day.

I decided to pop into a favourite shop and grab a quick coffee. While I was in the lineup to pay, my corporal came over the radio, asking if there was a female available to assist. I responded, saying that I would attend and asked what was going on.

"Just need a female here," was the reply.

It did not sound urgent and I was next in line, so I paid for my coffee and took it to go. Climbing back into my police car, I took a few moments to review the file details sent to my computer terminal. I absently sipped my coffee. My corporal had been dispatched to a residence in assistance to some personnel from the health authority. There was not much more than that noted in the dispatch ticket, so I really had no idea what was going on. I had been to these sorts of calls before. Usually they involved standing by and keeping the peace while an outpatient was encouraged to take their medication. Other times a police officer might need to help transport someone to the hospital. Really, not a big deal.

I donned my sunglasses and pulled smoothly into traffic. I was headed to a location quite a distance away and it was going take some time before I pulled up to the residence. After several minutes of driving, my corporal raised me on the radio.

"What's your location?" he asked.

I'd worked with this guy for a while, so I could tell he seemed a bit agitated.

"I'm still about five minutes away," I said. "Is everything okay there?"

"It's fine," he said.

I continued driving.

"Where are you?" he asked me again after a few minutes.

Okay, now I was getting concerned. Was this an emergency?

"Should I be coming lights and sirens?" I asked in all earnestness.

"No, no. It's fine." was the reply.

I asked for dispatch's opinion about the file. She told me my corporal had met two health authority personnel at a residence and gone inside several minutes prior to the first call for a female member. I continued to scene, driving a little faster than before. I was almost there.

In Richmond, the main residential area is laid out in a grid pattern with long, straight major roads serving as the boundaries. Within each major block are a number of smaller streets that snake and wind sometimes seemingly at random. You really have to know your way around. I drove within the block of the call, looking for my corporal's police car while keeping an eye on the house addresses.

"How much longer?" my corporal asked.

"Just looking for your car. Which house is it?"

I was starting to feel anxious. What was going on?

My corporal described a two level home. I located and parked next to his police car and ran up the street to the house.

"I'm here, where are you?" I asked.

"Inside! Inside!"

I cautiously opened the front door. The foyer was small and there was a steep staircase leading directly up to the second floor. I scanned the foyer and then looked up the stairs. I could see my corporal standing there, at the very top of the stairs. He was slightly turned away from me, facing a wall. He had his gaze fixed firmly on an electrical socket low on the wall.

I crept up the stairs, scanning the upper level as I went.

"What's going on?" I asked.

"Over there."

He pointed behind him, not shifting his gaze from the wall.

I climbed the final few stairs, reaching the landing. I then realized what was going on. There, in the living room, standing in full view of the large bay window was a very old, very naked woman. She had wild steely grey hair and more wrinkles and folds than I ever thought would be possible. I'd never seen anything like it. She stood there, arms crossed with a stern look on her face. Her clothes were neatly stacked on the floor next to the glass coffee table.

"What's going on?" I asked.

The old lady did not reply, but one of the health authority ladies standing in the nearby dinning room quickly told me the story. The old woman was an outpatient from the local hospital who was allowed to live in her own home as long as she continued to take the medications she needed to stay healthy. On that day, the health authority staff had come to the home to check up on her and confirm medication compliance. They had not expected anything to go wrong, but had asked for a police officer just in case they had to take the old woman to the hospital. Well, as it turned out, the old woman was not too keen on talking with the health authority staff and when my corporal stepped in to help escort her to the hospital, she had decided to show her displeasure by getting naked.

I called the old woman by name.

"Okay," I said in a calm and soothing voice. "It is time to take a ride in my police car."

I slowly approached the old woman. Hopefully, I'd be able to just convince her to put her clothes back on. But before I'd taken two steps towards her, she turned and ran to the window!

"Whoooooooooooooo!" She shouted, arms outstretched, shaking every little wrinkle for the world outside to see.

I rushed over and took hold of her left wrist with just the index finger and thumb of my left hand. Trying my best to touch as little of her as possible, I guided her to the ground using the simplest of techniques taught at Depot. On the way down, I realized I'd forgotten about that coffee table. I yanked her out of the way at the last moment, praying she would not break a hip or something when we hit the shag carpeting.

"You good?" came the voice of my corporal.

I could not see him from where I was on the floor, but I imagined that he was still watching that electrical outlet.

"Yeah. You wanna get me a blanket or something?"

I ducked as a patchwork quilt came sailing through the air like a matador's cape.

We got the old lady sorted out and I transported her to the hospital in the back of my police car. My corporal said it would be best if we never spoke of this again. I agreed. Of course, he never said anything about writing.

THE HOME TEAM
Constable April Dequanne

As I travelled from Toronto, Ontario to Whale Cove, Nunavut, I was progressively awakened to the reality of what I had gotten myself into. It was just a month-long posting, to relieve a Mountie in Whale Cove who was going on vacation. But after a series of connections between Toronto and Whale Cove, the passengers on my flight transformed from business, to casual, to what looked like the cast of *Never Cry Wolf*. Massive goose down coats, huge boots, and real fur hoods were the norm. The plane I was on was travelling ahead of a winter storm, and for the leg into Rankin Inlet the pilot told us that he was going to "chance it." *Excuse me?*

Safely on the ground at last, I zipped up my fancy Gortex jacket and popped a toque on my head. With confidence in my high-tech gear, I exited the plane for the fifty yard dash across the tarmac to the terminal. In that short time, the wind managed to freeze the moist air around my mouth and nose, even the tiny hairs on my face. It froze my tearing eyes shut and blew right through my jacket.

A man walked by and whispered, "Fight nature with nature."

I turned to see the man who spoke this wisdom but he didn't stop. He was dressed in a sealskin jacket with a hood trimmed in fox fur, a pair of tall moccasins (*kamiks*), and polar bear fur mitts.

With the culture and environment shock behind me, I settled into my work. I enjoyed exploring and discovering the people and environment of Whale Cove. The people were very welcoming and I had several local experiences I will remember my entire life. I was invited out on snowmobile trips. I witnessed the pride and generosity of two hunters who brought their kill (three musk ox) back to share with their neighbours. I was humbled to witness that in a community where food was incredibly expensive, the instinct to share was still so strong. I also got to see the kids enjoy the stuffed animals that had been donated by the people who worked in my home detachment. For many of those kids, the donated stuffed animals were the only toys they had.

One afternoon, Tom, the gym teacher from Inuglak School, called and asked if I would be interested in taking his place in a hockey game that night. After hibernating for three weeks, I welcomed the exercise. Tom's equipment was a good fit except for the gloves, helmet, and skates. I began to ask some of the kids who were hanging around the arena for the required items.

Surprised, many of them asked, "You gonna play hockey?" and offered up their gear.

Eight-year-old Paul Qiok had just the right size skates and helmet for me. I put on the gear and laced up the skates in the foyer of the arena, as there was no change room available to me.

The young boys and girls gathered around and filled the remaining time with questions:

"You gonna play with the guys?"

"You ever play hockey before?"

"Why are you playing hockey?"

"Are you afraid?"

"Can you skate?"

They had never seen a girl play hockey before.

The "Home" team looked young and strong. They were a group of guys who had grown up together, surviving the harsh climate and playing one of the few sports available to them. Our "Visiting" team, with the help of some locals, was not so young and strong, and not as acclimatized to the harsh climate and way of life. I stepped on the ice and skated to blend in with everyone during the warm-up.

The ice surface was cold and fast. No artificial ice there, it was the real thing. The players sharpened their skates by hand and got their hockey equipment during trips out of the community. With the bare essentials, these kids grew up playing Canada's sport the way it started, and with skills that would shame even some of the best hockey players I know. I figured that many were just waiting to be discovered. In fact, it had happened to Jordin Tootoo, from nearby Rankin Inlet, who now played in the NHL.

When I stepped on the ice I thought I was playing against the Nashville Predators. Many were wearing hand-me-down jerseys or NHL replica jerseys with Tootoo (#22) on their backs. It was evident that Tootoo was a local hero.

It was not long before word spread and the arena started to fill with spectators. They were there to see if a girl could actually play hockey. The puck dropped, and in the face-off circle I saw him—a bootlegger from the community who was the bane of my existence and the subject of many calls to duty while I had been in Whale Cove. He was on the young and strong team.

I'm going to get creamed, I thought as we made brief eye contact.

I kept my head up and stayed clear of the corners—I had never stepped on the ice with a guy I had arrested before. He was young, strong and quick and knew how to handle the puck. Just days earlier, when I had arrested him, I had the upper hand with my training and "tools" of the job. Now, I felt uncomfortably vulnerable as the playing field was heavily tilted in his favour. I had stepped onto *his* ice.

The game was fast paced and the opposition had no idea a girl was playing. That made me feel like I was holding my own out there. I even took a couple of hits, picked myself up, and kept skating. The score was six to four for the Home team. We seized the chance for a breakaway during a bad line change by the Home team. From my left wing, I dipped quickly to the middle near centre ice, and found the puck on my stick. I skated with all I had toward the net. This was my chance to contribute to the score. I could hear the cold ice being split behind me by the blades of what I hoped was a teammate. He skated past me, tapped my stick, and tried to grab the puck. I fought hard to keep the puck, dipped left, and fired the shot from the top of the face off circle just before I took the hit. The puck hit the goalie's stick, popped up between his pads, and trickled into the net. The crowd cheered and "oohed."

From my crumpled position on the ice I celebrated the goal, and grabbed the hand that offered to pick me up. It was him, my work-life nemesis.

"Lucky shot," he said and skated away.

We were losing, but it was okay because the crowd was cheering. They were chanting my name! Girls, women, boys, and men alike were chanting *my* name every time I stepped on the ice. I felt like Jordin Tootoo, a local hero.

After the game, in the comfort of my apartment, I iced a bruise that I decided I would not tell anyone about. A knock on the door made me jump. My apartment was connected to the detachment and it could have been an emergency. I opened the door and it was him.

"You did really great out there, and I just want you to have this."

He handed me a sweaty jersey which had been covered in cologne to mask the smell. On the front was the image of an inukshuk.

"We play again next Thursday, if you want," he said.

When my temporary posting was over, I arrived back in Toronto on a Wednesday, late in the evening. I exited the plane in boots and heavy winter jacket. I realized that many people on my connecting flight from Ottawa were looking at me inquisitively. I had refused to remove my layers of clothing. I had earned bragging rights, and I wanted people to know that I had just returned from a part of Canada's most beautiful North. Assunai Whale Cove.

FLIGHT
Constable Sarah Leslie

It was the Fall of 2008 and my evening had started off just as I had come to expect, being posted to the Vancouver International Airport Detachment in Richmond, British Columbia. I took a sip of my venti sized coffee, reflecting that it was unfortunate that this particular drink did not come in a larger size. I noticed a definite nip in the evening air which suggested that winter was just around the corner. The cold was the perfect contrast to my steaming hot coffee. The night promised to be one of diverse extremes. The bright lights and warmth of the terminal during foot patrols would contrast with checks of vehicles conducted at an unlit and cold beach nearby. Quiet streets and hours of silence on the radio would be punctuated by police officers calling in status updates generated by proactive work.

I was dressed in my uniform, driving a marked patrol vehicle, looking for anything out of the ordinary. "Ordinary" is not very common in this line of work, and you never know what you may encounter on any given patrol.

Early into my shift, I received a call from two co-workers who were working in plain clothes and had noticed an individual who appeared to be out of place. The male was apparently dressed to the nines, yet he was collecting used cigarette butts from the ashtrays outside the terminal. Another contrast. I headed up to the terminal to check it out.

When I arrived at the scene, my co-worker surreptitiously pointed out the suspicious man and I nonchalantly approached him. He was wearing pressed slacks and a suit jacket. He appeared to be clean and well groomed. Although picking up cigarette butts is not necessarily an illegal activity, the spirit of proactive policing suggested that I should take a closer look. I had no preconceived ideas about him. It was possible that he might be very well off and just didn't mind the odd used cigarette or two. Perhaps saving money on a nico-tine addiction was how he'd made his millions. I speculated that such a gen-tleman would surely be morbidly embarrassed if his money-saving scheme were to be discovered. Maybe that was why he had travelled all the way to the airport to engage in the activity. On the other hand, the man might be strug-gling financially, or even homeless. It could be entirely possible that his taste in fine clothing (and who knows what else) had cleaned out his bank account and he was now relegated to picking up used smokes just to get by.

I decided to strike up a conversation by simply asking the man what he was doing at the airport. He appeared reasonable and articulate, casually telling me that he flew regularly and was waiting for some flight mainte-nance to be completed. I determined that he was a pilot.

Prior to joining the RCMP, I'd spent several years surrounded by air-craft and aviation personnel. I had taken two years of flight school as a youth and had worked at numerous military bases across Canada as a young adult. Following my acceptance into the RCMP, I had contin-ued to serve as a reservist in the Canadian Armed Forces, Air Element. I therefore felt a sense of embarrassment on behalf of this pilot, having caught him in such an unbecoming act. I quickly shifted the subject to the weather that evening, the approaching Christmas season, and anything else I could think of in the moment. For his part, the male was polite and transitioned easily as we continued our conversation.

Although this man struck me as odd, I decided my time could best be used back out on patrol. After all, it is not illegal to smoke another man's used cigarettes. I asked him for his pilot license so that we both could be on our way. But the male ignored my request, continuing on with our con-versation as if I had not said anything at all. I asked him a second time. The male advised me that he did not have his license with him but that it was "near by." He again told me that he was waiting for flight maintenance.

I was clearly getting nowhere so I decided to change my approach. It was only then that the conversation transitioned from casual to peculiar. I asked the male how long he thought he'd have to wait at the airport. He admitted that he didn't know how long it would take to repair his ship.

I was almost lost for words. "Ship?" I asked.

"Yes," the male said casually. "I told you, my spaceship is being repaired."

I stood there dumbfounded, which was a first for me and has not hap-pened since. The male took advantage of my silence to clarify his flight plan. He told me he was headed to "the galaxies."

I found my voice again and asked the male for his name. He matter-of-factually stated that it was Lord Sekhmet. Although my knowledge of ancient history was limited to the basics, I was fairly certain that he had just identified himself as an Ancient Egyptian deity.

It was cold and the airport was a fair distance away from the city. The man, whoever he was, had no reasonable way to make his way home (if such a place even existed). I wanted to make sure he would be safe and could care for himself.

"Well, Mr. Sekhmet," I cheerfully said. "I'm currently on my way to the hospital. Would you care to join me?"

Mr. Sekhmet said yes and willingly got into the rear of my police vehicle. Still, my co-workers stood nearby, ensuring all was well.

It was not until I had settled in the driver's seat and closed my door that Mr. Sekhmet's behaviour changed. It was like I was dealing with an entirely different individual. He swore at me and threatened both my family and I. I was called every bad word I knew and I think I even learned some new ones. Mr. Sekhmet told me he had been flying his space ship longer than I had been alive.

"And how long is that, exactly?" I asked him.

"Since 10,000 BC," he told me.

The drive to the hospital that night felt like the longest I'd ever taken. All the threats, cursing and violent gestures I observed through the rear-view mirror reminded me of how important it is not to become complacent. What had started out as a cute and even humorous conversation with a seemingly harmless individual had turned into a disturbing and almost frightening experience. This file became a valuable lesson for me. People are unpredictable. Attitudes can shift within a split second.

The man eventually calmed down and was given the care he needed at a local hospital. Despite all the verbal abuse and threats I'd received, I really did feel kind of bad for him. Who knew how he had come to be in the circumstances in which I had found him. He could be anyone's brother, father or son. At the end of the day, I knew I had done the right thing and that he was in good hands.

While typing my report in the hospital parking lot, I grabbed my coffee and took a big sip. It was as cold as the night air. On any other night I would have re-heated it, but this time, I simply smirked and drank it cold.

ZONE PARTNERS
Corporal Donna Morse, née Burns (Ret.)

In the municipality where I worked thirty years ago, there was only one other officer assigned to my zone. He and I worked alone, each of us driving our own police cruiser. There were other members who worked the same shift, but all were assigned to cover different areas within the large sprawling municipality. I loved patrolling my assigned zone and liked working with my partner. The variance of calls kept us both busy and made our jobs interesting.

My partner was junior to me in service but very enthusiastic, capable and hardworking. We had worked together for a number of months and had established a good rapport. There was an ease in the working relationship and we both knew that we had each other's back.

One Saturday evening, my partner and I prepared for work expecting a busy night shift. It was a normal fall day on the west coast with winds, rain and a bone penetrating dampness in the air.

The evening started out as expected and I was dispatched to several complaints. After one routine file, I returned to my vehicle just in time to hear dispatch calling for my partner and I. It was only two hours into the shift and I assumed my partner was busy, so I responded, advising that I would take the new file.

I was asked to attend a motor vehicle accident reported at a location approximately five kilometres from where I was. There was no report of injury so I headed up to the scene at a normal rate of speed without engaging the lights and sirens.

It was extremely dark that night and the area was unlit. When I arrived at the scene, I saw a truck laying on its side. There was a man sitting outside the vehicle, holding his head. I saw a number of other vehicles stopped on the roadway and people who had stopped to help were milling around in the area.

I parked my police vehicle and approached the man to determine if he was hurt. He told me he had been the only one in the truck and that he was fine, but to me he seemed groggy.

I heard people calling out, "Over here! Over here!"

I couldn't really see who they were. I left the man at the truck and walked across the road towards where I had heard the shouting and realized that there was another vehicle lying in the deep ditch.

Two males intercepted me on my way over to the second vehicle. One said he was a doctor. Standing on either side of me, they each gently took hold of an arm.

"There's nothing you can do for him," the doctor said.

I had no idea what he was talking about and shook off their hold, continuing towards the vehicle in the ditch.

I did not immediately recognize the vehicle as a police cruiser as the light bar was no longer attached to the roof and the entire vehicle was scraped and crushed.

I continued down into the ditch and found my partner, slumped over the steering wheel, unconscious and bleeding from the head. The front portion of the roof had crushed inwards into his head and the dashboard and steering wheel had been pushed into his chest.

I called for emergency medical support and enlisted the other people in the area to block off the road. Then I stayed with my partner, encouraging him and hoping for some response. I refused to give up on him. It seemed to take forever for the other police officers and paramedics to arrive. In situations like this, time seems to stand still.

My partner was rushed to the hospital and the driver of the pickup was arrested for impaired driving. It turned out that he had actually been arrested for the same charge just the week before by one of our watch members. He had numerous impaired driving convictions and arrests but thirty years ago the penalties for impaired driving were not as severe as they are today.

My partner was hospitalized for many months and, initially, it was uncertain whether he would even survive. But he fought with courage and perseverance to cope with the traumatic injuries he had sustained. Although I have lost contact with him over the years, I think of him often and sincerely hope he is still fighting the fight. He was a true inspiration to all of us.

MAQUA THE BEAR
Inspector Jim Potts (Ret.), Elder

The RCMP training academy is called "Depot Division." People in the know pronounce it with a slight French accent so that it sounds like "Deh-poh." How you say it will quickly identify you as either being associated to the RCMP, or not.

RCMP recruits are called "cadets" and they form classes called "troops" while going through the process of earning their place within the regular member ranks of the RCMP.

The process of transforming from cadet to regular member is long and incremental. Progress is easily discernable by the type of uniform a troop wears: junior troops are in cargo pants and running shoes; moderately senior troops wear full RCMP "duty" uniform complete with a forge cap and gun belt called a "Sam Black." The most senior troops can be seen wearing the RCMP's iconic high brown boots and Stetson hat. Sometimes, the senior troops wear the full scarlet Red Serge.

If you ever visit Depot, stand outside the dining hall (also known as the Mess Hall or simply "the Mess"). Right before lunch you will see a swell of cadets arriving wearing all sorts of different uniforms. You might even be able to overhear their excited stories from the morning as they break ranks and swarm in for food.

I love stories, and Depot is prime story breeding ground with its own costumes, language, traditions and energy. Stories are everything there and they are told every day by almost everyone. Cadets tell stories from home; Instructors tell stories from the field; Scenario players tell fictional stories to create learning opportunities. Spoken histories, traditions and expectations are very much alive at Depot.

The Depot grounds are sacred too, full of their own stories. The chapel which stands at one end of the parade square is the oldest building in Saskatchewan. Inside are the reminders of who the RCMP used to be. Stained glass windows commemorate fallen members. The fading retired Guidon, the old banner of the RCMP, is left there in its final hanging position, like it's watching over history itself.

Just a few feet away from the chapel is the place where Louis Riel was executed, forever polarizing Depot as a place of intrigue and infamy in Canadian history. Across the parade square is the RCMP cenotaph which bears the names of the Mounties who have fallen in the line of duty since 1873. Their stories are told often by the people who knew them and are remembered by their RCMP descendants through ceremony and history. The canon carriage that sat on the Drill Hall vestibule, one of the only surviving of its kind, saw its day in the March West and was used to bring the remains of the Canadian Unknown Soldier to rest at the monument in Ottawa.

One day I received the great responsibility and honour to add a story to the patchwork quilt of Depot's oral history. But before I explain that, it is worth describing a little bit about cadet life, particularly the gender division at Depot.

Individual identity, to some degree, fades away at Depot. You live in a dorm where phone calls, changing clothes, showering, eating, homework et cetera... are a Troop affair. Women and men have separate accommodations of course, but with so much of Depot life playing out in the dorms, women can become the unseen minority. Add to this the intentional de-individualization thanks to the uniforms and marching, I expect a woman's individual story can be hard to hear in the buzz of what Depot is. That is why when I was asked by a group of RCMP cadet women to share with them what I felt to be the most important lesson from my policing career I immediately thought of a spiritual story passed on through time by the Elders. As a man, as an RCMP Veteran and an Elder myself, I couldn't think of a more perfect time and place to share the spiritual story of Maqua The Bear:

> One day, Maqua sent word to all the animal children that he would hold a feast on the night of the full moon. He would build a fire. There would be lots to eat, dancing, singing and laughter. All were invited to come.
>
> The first night of the full moon, Maqua built his great fire and upon seeing the glow in the sky the animal chil-

dren came from near and far. There was indeed a lot to eat. There was dancing, singing and much laughter and everyone was having a good time.

Now, animal children like to have grease on their food, like you and I like to have butter on our bread and gravy on our potatoes. But there was no grease. Soon the animal children complained, "Maqua, your food is good but it is dry. We like to have grease on our food."

"You want grease on you food you shall have grease on you food," said Maqua.

Maqua began to dance around the fire and sing his own magic song. As he sang he rubbed his paws together over the fire. The flames licked his paws. There is much fat under a bear's skin and it started to melt and drip from his paws. The animal children came with bowls and caught the grease, passing it out and now everyone was happy.

Meanwhile, Jay, a bird, was listening and watching from high in a tree. Jay wanted to do what Maqua was doing. He listened carefully and memorized Maqua's magic song. Soon, Jay sent word to all the animal children that he too was going to have a great fire, and all should come for there will be dancing, singing, laughter and much to eat. He assured them that all would have a good time.

When the day came, Jay built his fire and all the animal children came. Again there was dancing, singing, laughter and much to eat. Soon, some of the animal children cried out, "Jay your food is good but it is dry, we like to have grease on our food!"

"You want grease on your food you shall have grease on your food," said Jay.

With that, he began to dance around the fire. As he danced he remembered Maqua's magic song. As he sang he flapped his wings, put his feet out over the fire and rubbed them together. But the Creator was watching. And as Jay sang Maqua's song, the Creator became angry. He caused the flames to go up and burn Jay's feet and Jay fell back from the fire squawking and hopping. To this day, if you look at a Jay's feet you will see that they are charcoal grey and that he doesn't walk, but must hop because he was burned by that fire.

The Creator was angry with Jay not because he held a feast or built a great fire, but because he had been singing Maqua's song and not his own. There is no magic when you sing someone else's song.

Maqua teaches us that we all, male or female, must find the magic in being ourselves. As I told that group of RCMP cadet women that day, "The magic is in being you and being the unique police officer that the Creator made *you* to be. With your own dance, with your own song, and most of all, with your own story."

PENELOPE P. ENROUTE TO MARKET
Chief Superintendent Ruby Burns (Ret.)

While on patrol one bright sunny day in Manitoba, I received a call to attend a nice Ukrainian woman's farm. There was a report that a trespasser was causing a lot of damage in the front garden. I attended right away. Every Ukrainian I'd met up to that point had kept an excellent garden and I wanted to prevent as much damage as I could.

I met with the complainant down the road from her home and she provided a description of the suspect: she was large, she was fat and she was … pink? That's right, there was a pig in her garden! The hungry sow had eaten all of the petunias, a large portion of the rose bushes and most of the pansies. All that eating must have exhausted her, because she had now settled in for a nap. The lady told me she wanted her removed from the premises (if I didn't mind).

I took a look at the garden and noted the damage caused by the hungry pig. And there was Penelope, as I decided that she should be called, lying quietly against the corner of the farmhouse, enjoying a nice afternoon siesta. The lady told me she had no idea where Penelope had come from and didn't recognize her as a local resident. From a distance, Penelope appeared to be a fine looking pig, maybe even cute, and I decided that she was someone's wayward prized sow. I radioed my dispatcher to check the police databases, hoping that someone had reported her missing. But sadly, no one had.

I asked my dispatcher to telephone a local veterinarian to attend the farm, examine Penelope and transport her from the property. The veterinarian said he was unable to come out to the farmhouse but would gladly examine the pig if I could transport her to his clinic. No simple task, but I was up to the challenge.

As a child, I'd read somewhere that one could lead a pig by laying down a trail of rolled oats. I personally wasn't too familiar with farms or farm animals but I had friends who lived on a farm. Maybe it had been one of them who had told me this advice. Actually, I couldn't remember exactly where I'd heard about pigs and rolled oats, but it seemed worth the shot. I jumped into my police vehicle and headed to a nearby convenience store to purchase some.

My plan was simple. I was driving the company suburban, which conveniently had several sheets of plywood in the back. What could be easier? I had lay the trail of rolled oats leading from Penelope to the suburban where I would use the plywood as a make-shift ramp. Penelope would literally walk herself into my vehicle. No lifting required! Then, I would take a trip to the veterinarian for Penelope's examination, where they would declare her to be the finest pig they had ever seen and offer to house her, (free of charge, of course), until the owner was located. Pig and owner (a vegetarian, of course) would be reunited and everyone would live happily ever after.

At the convenience store, I loaded my arms with several bags of rolled oats. The store keeper manning the cash register raised his eyebrows and asked why I was purchasing so many bags. I smiled and explained about Penelope napping in the Ukrainian lady's garden and described my plan for the rolled oats trail. Two gentlemen in their mid-twenties shopping in the store overheard my story and eagerly volunteered to assist me. They were keenly interested in my investigation and practically begged me to let them come along to rouse Penelope from her garden nap. I finally agreed to the offer of help. As I pulled out some cash to pay for my purchase, the store keeper waived me off. He told me it was on the house, for Penelope.

I returned to the scene armed with several bags of rolled oats. My two young helpers followed in their pickup truck. At the garden, we sprung into action, opening up the bags of rolled oats and preparing the make-shift ramp of plywood at the back of my suburban. I then began laying a trail of oats from the suburban to the pig. But as I approached Penelope, she became agitated. The closer I got, the worse she became. She tossed her head back and forth, making a guttural sound. As I got closer, she struggled to stand. That's when I noticed the blood. Penelope had severe injuries to her hindquarters. As she struggled and failed to rise on all four trotters, I suddenly realized that she was not the cute "little piggy" I'd initially thought she was. I estimated that Penelope tipped the scales around 400 pounds—that was my conservative guess. The way Penelope had been laying against the corner of the house, half-hidden by a bush, had camouflaged both her injuries and her true size. And now, there was so much blood. Penelope retreated against the house, spraying blood onto the siding, each time she thrashed about.

I stood in that garden with a handful of rolled oats cupped in one hand, and a half empty bag in the other, and realized that my plan was not going to work. The only humane thing to do would be to put Penelope out of her misery as quickly as possible.

Under the Animal Husbandry Act I needed two witnesses to verify that Penelope was severely injured and needed to be put down. My two new gentlemen friends stepped up to the plate and verified this for me, signing the required form. After this, they departed the scene.

Almost immediately after my two helpers had left, two highway patrol men arrived on the scene. My partners had heard the initial call on the police radio and were curious about how I was making out. They surveyed the scene and agreed that Penelope had to be put down. We flipped a coin to decide who would shoot the pig and who would comfort the Ukrainian woman. Fate decided that I should advise the elderly Ukrainian woman to stay in her house and not be afraid when she heard the noise of gunfire. Penelope was badly injured and had to be put down. She understood.

Penelope was put out of her misery as quickly and humanely as possible. The two highway patrol men left, but my work was far from over. I called for a municipal vehicle to remove Penelope from the garden and take her to her final resting spot. Her body would likely be taken to the municipal landfill, but I liked to think that her soul was in Piggy Heaven.

After this, I found a garden hose and, for the next two hours, sprayed and scrubbed Penelope's blood from the side of the Ukrainian woman's white-painted farmhouse. A few days later, I returned, off-duty, to help replant the garden.

I managed to identify Penelope's owner and learned that she had not been a prize sow going to competition, but rather was food-stock en-route to a slaughterhouse in Winnipeg. The tailgate of Penelope's transport vehicle had malfunctioned and she had tumbled onto the highway. She escaped the slaughterhouse but her taste of freedom had been marred by her critical injuries. Still, Penelope had managed to make her way to the Ukrainian woman's garden where she enjoyed a final meal of petunias, roses and pansies before settling in for her last long nap.

This event happened when I was still a rookie. At that time, I was extremely keen to learn police work. I wanted to arrest every bad guy and throw him in jail. I wanted to participate in high-speed chases and solve homicides. I wanted to sprint before I could walk. Penelope's file taught me a lot. It was a simple matter with no adrenaline, publicity or bragging rights involved. The Ukrainian woman was deeply upset about the damage to her garden and needed help dealing with the pig who had taken up temporary residence in it. Meanwhile, the two young gentlemen were sincerely interested in lending a hand to their neighbour. And the storekeeper contributed in the best way he could by donating the rolled oats. Penelope's file was a demonstration of teamwork and camaraderie.

Many of the guys teased me unmercifully about Penelope's file, but I was still always thankful it came my way. When someone asks me to tell them about my favourite investigation I often begin with "well there was the file when 'this little piggy' didn't quite make it to market."

Penelope's file taught me how much the public rely on the RCMP for assistance on unique issues. It also taught me how much we rely on the public to support us in our investigations. I hung onto these lessons and they became crucial building blocks for my handling of the major cases I worked on later in my career. Never underestimate the general public. The majority are ready, willing and able to lend us a hand. Throughout the 35 plus years of my career, members of the general public have assisted me by providing valuable information that has resulted in the successful solving of assaults, break and enters, arsons and even homicides. And they've helped in numerous other ways. One afternoon, several drivers stopped to assist as I wrestled with a drunk on a four lane highway. And near the end of my career, a local resident stopped by the perimeter we'd set up while dealing with an ongoing critical incident to deliver us coffee. The note he left read *For your long hours ahead.*

We need the assistance of the public just as much as they need us. Whether the support comes through assistance during routine or serious investigations, random acts of kindness or the outpouring of support when members of our RCMP family are killed in the line of duty, it is often jaw dropping and always genuinely appreciated. Thank you all!

A WELL TAILORED MAN
Constable Adriana Peralta, née O'Malley

Depot Division in Regina has been home to the RCMP Cadet Training Program since 1885. Although certain aspects of the programming have changed in keeping with the times, the rigorous training and high level of performance expected of recruits have remained constant. No matter what year they joined the Force, at which posting they first served, or what rank they have or may later achieve, almost every Mountie has passed through the hallowed halls of Depot.

At Depot, cadets are exposed to the various realities of policing. Whether it's firearms, physical training, or the legal application of the law, preparing recruits for "the real world" of policing is the main focus of the instructors. An integral part of the Depot experience is scenario-based training. Depot is set up like a small town complete with houses, labeled streets, a hockey arena and even its very own police detachment. Over the course of their training, cadets conduct mock investigations, taking turns playing the role of police officer, victim, witness and suspect at various locations around the base. There might be a domestic at one of the prefab homes or a fight at the arena. Every now and then, a local gang of graffiti artists runs wild, tagging everything in sight. Sometimes the corner store gets robbed. Considering the number of future police officers wandering around the base at any given time, you might expect Depot to have a much lower crime rate. But, never fail, each week there is a new rash of crimes ready for eager recruits to investigate. Of course, everyone smiles and chuckles during these investigations. This is in part due to the fact that sleep-deprived troop mates serving as actors tend to feel a little mischievous. Depending on how they are employed, wigs, oversized clothing and other miscellaneous items borrowed from

Depot's prop room can bring either a sense of reality or levity to a file. But despite any minor shenanigans, the ultimate goal of each cadet is to gain the skills necessary to leave the surreal crime world of Depot behind and enter the real world of policing where solving crimes has a true affect on people's lives.

When I left Depot, I was posted to Richmond, British Columbia as a general duty police officer. My job was to deal with various emergency and non-emergency calls for service. As I was posted to a mid-sized city, I had the luxury of working closely with a training officer for approximately four months. During the time that we worked together, my trainer took responsibility for ensuring that I was truly prepared to be a frontline investigator. One of the ways he did this was by exposing me to every type of investigation possible. During those four months I went from call to call, never quite knowing what was to come. Consequently, this was a period of "firsts." I investigated my first vehicle collision, attended my first assault and conducted my first next of kin notification. I am proud of many things that occurred during that time and have a number of fond memories. There is one case in particular, though, that I will be recounting well past the end of my career.

I will never forget the call. It was a night shift and I was riding with a different trainer as mine was away. Around 1 a.m. or so, our dispatcher broadcasted over the radio, looking for an available unit to assist at a care facility for seniors. Our dispatcher relayed that a care aid was seeking assistance with a resident who was causing a disturbance. My trainer looked at me and indicated I should respond and advise the dispatcher that I would take the call. With a nod and grin, my trainer said I would be taking the lead on this investigation. I naively mistook this to mean that he had great confidence in my abilities. In reality, I suspect he had been to this place before and knew what was to come.

When we arrived at the care home, we were immediately buzzed in via the secured front door. We were greeted by a rather exasperated looking care aid who advised that she was at her "wits end" with "that man." We learned that the care aid had been trying to get an elderly resident to take his medication and go to bed but that he was simply refusing to follow any of her directions.

As the care aid recounted the events that had transpired over the previous couple of hours, a rather stately looking elderly man came marching towards us. As he approached, he expressed his pleasure in seeing the police. As it turned out, he was in need of some help. The gentleman reported that thieves were running amuck and needed to be stopped. Glaring at the care aid, he advised me that he was positive that "that woman" had something to do with it. I noticed that both the care aid and elderly man had referred to each other as "that" individual. This indicated to me that my chances of finding a resolution that was satisfactory to both parties was close to nil. Despite this, I persevered in the hopes of demonstrating my capabilities to my trainer.

As the elderly man continued talking with me, I learned that his upset stemmed from a pair of missing pants. The file was starting to sound a bit strange, but knowing that the end goal was to get the elderly man settled in his room, I went with it and requested that he take us to the scene of the crime. My elderly victim obligingly agreed and led the way down the hallway.

While showing me to his room, my elderly victim reported that his khaki coloured pair of pants had mysteriously disappeared after being sent for washing.

To prove his point, he flung open his closet door and exclaimed, "You see? My pants are gone."

I peered into the closet and observed a row of neatly hung khaki coloured pants. After a beat or two of silence I asked the man exactly how many pairs of khaki coloured pants he owned.

"Seven, of course! One for each day of the week," he explained.

A quick count revealed that there were precisely seven pairs of khaki pants hung in his closet. I started to think that my elderly victim was not actually a victim of theft. Perhaps he was just a bit confused.

But as I formulated what to say next, he pulled one pair off of a hanger and said, "You see? These ones. They don't fit."

Taking the pants in hand, I looked at the inside of the waistband and, as quick as that, I had it solved. At the time, my grandfather (may he rest in peace) was living in a similar type of care facility so I knew the laundry was done en-mass. Every resident was required to write their name on the inside of their clothing to ensure it was returned to the right person. Of course, that didn't always happen. Indeed, I discovered that written on the inside of these troublesome pants was another man's name. No theft here.

As it turned out, solving the crime was the easy part. Having my elderly victim accept my explanation was another matter entirely. Despite my best efforts, he would not accept that "that woman" had not been involved in a conspiracy to rob him of his pants. As I persisted in my attempts to assuage his concerns and explain the situation, he suddenly decided that he was none too pleased with the quality of service he was receiving from police. He expressed this displeasure by flopping down onto his bed, sticking his arms straight out in front of himself and demanding that I take him to jail.

"But you haven't committed a crime," I said, attempting to reason with him.

"I don't care what for. Just take me to jail," he retorted.

I felt laughter building up inside. This seemingly ordinary file now bore an element of shenaniganism strikingly similar to that as I'd experienced in a number of my Depot scenarios. Biting my cheek and spinning around, I gave a quick nod to my trainer and left the room. Yes, I had to admit defeat in regards to convincing the elderly man of my point of view, but I figured that was better than bursting out laughing right there in his room.

I took some pride in the fact that I had managed to solve what I now affectionately refer to as "the case of the missing pants." As for my trainer, he somehow convinced the man to stay in his room for the rest of the night. Back in the patrol car that laughter I'd managed to keep inside came out in full force. Those pesky missing pants proved to be a good comedic interlude for the rest of that shift and well beyond.

To the elderly gentleman I extend my thanks and appreciation. I'm sure he never knew the impact he had on that newbie constable. Even after 10 years, thinking of him and those missing pants still puts a smile on my face and elicits a hearty chuckle. In a job that can be daunting at times, those laughs are definitely priceless.

THE QUEST
Corporal Veronica S.E. Fox

Time: 3:30 p.m.
My last night shift of the block is upon me as I rub sleep from my eyes. It is summer and so unbelievably hot that I had to sleep with my window open and fan on. This meant that as I "slept" through the day, I was able to hear every joyful exclamation from the kids next door as they made good use of the new trampoline their parents purchased for their summer vacation. Thankfully, the kids took a break while I still had a good three hours of scheduled sleeping time left. That was when their dad decided to mow the lawn.

I reach for the glass of water I keep by my bedside. The ice melted hours ago and it's now tepid. I drink it anyhow and get ready to leave for work.

Time: 5:15 p.m.
I had pulled off a decent workout at the detachment gym despite a less than ideal commute to the office. The air conditioner in my 1991 Ford Tempo busted at the beginning of my 45 minute commute so I had to stop by a drive-thru and order a blended iced drink just to survive the trip. By the time I got to the detachment, my icy drink was melted and nasty in its plastic cup and I had managed to sweat through my shirt into the fabric of the car seat. The only positive to the whole ordeal was that, as I'd commuted in my workout clothes, everyone in the gym thought I had gone for a run outside before hitting the gym. That's right, I'm hard-core that way.

Time: 5:20 p.m.
The detachment showers appear to be all out of hot water. Despite the afore-mentioned heat wave, this does not make for an enjoyable showering experi-

ence. I put on my uniform, but before donning all the associated equipment, I empty my bladder for what I believe may be the last time for the next twelve hours of my shift. Of course I never *hope* to go half a day or more without a bathroom break, but I'm always prepared that this might be a reality.

As a female police officer, I'm used to not being able to use a bathroom whenever the fancy takes me. My personal best is 16.5 hours. Using a public toilet—assuming you can find one—is a lengthy and complicated process for a female in police uniform. The duty belt is kind of like taking your purse to the bathroom, except you obviously would never hang your gun belt up on the stall door hook. To be fair, you really shouldn't put your purse there, either. I never put my gun belt on the ground as I'm terrified anyone could snatch it out from under the door. Aside from the obvious public and officer safety risk that would pose, how embarrassing would it be for me to have to run out of a bathroom and into a crowded restaurant while holding my pants up and chasing the bad guy who just snatched my belt? So what's left? Well ladies: What do you do with your purse if you're not using the hook? Hang it around your neck, of course! Did I mention that the whole thing weighs around 30 pounds? Try keeping that off the ground while simultaneously not touching the toilet seat. And that's in a normal bathroom. Don't even get me started on my past experiences with port-a-potties.

Time: 6:00 p.m.
Briefing—It seems that I am the only female member working tonight. Our Watch Commander wants the boys and me to fit a roadblock into our other duties this evening. It has been sunny and hot and it is Friday night so we are bound to catch a number of impaired drivers. Prepared for a busy night, we head out of briefing and load our duty bags into our cars. My police car has almost a half tank of gas. There's no way it will last the whole shift. I plan to refuel at the first gas station I see. But first, I need coffee.

Time: 6:20 p.m.
I am totally dragging this evening, but I'm torn between my desperate need for caffeine and the knowledge that whatever fluid I consume will have an impact on me later in the shift. Coffee always makes me have to pee. When my fatigue wins out, I order a medium iced coffee. I'm about five minutes into a conversation with my teammates when our dispatcher announces that an emergency has occurred. A man is reporting that

someone is breaking into his home. We all rush to our vehicles to attend the file. I end up chugging my drink on the way to scene.

Time: 8:43 p.m.
The "break and enter" in progress file was actually a "we're here to steal your illegal marijuana" in progress file. The victim in this case was a guy who had been operating an illegal grow-op out of his two story residence. A group of males had stormed his house and taken most of his product. He called police in a panic only to be arrested for drug production. That's what they call irony.

After we clear the residence and arrest the sole occupant, (the hapless home owner/pot grower), our team disperses. One member heads back to cells with the prisoner while another returns to the office to write up the warrant. The remaining members perform a few neighbourhood inquiries before going back out on patrol. Meanwhile, I stay behind to secure the scene.

While sitting in my police vehicle, I begin to feel the effects of that coffee and think maybe I should not have had any after all. If only I'd been assigned prisoner transport or warrant writing for this file. At least then I'd have been able to visit the detachment bathroom by now. I tell myself there's no point in thinking about it. Yet as I sit in the driver's seat, twisted towards my computer to type a report, my duty belt presses uncomfortably into my bladder.

10:46 p.m.
When the boys come back to execute the warrant, I take the opportunity to visit the toilet inside the grow-op. But one look at the state of the bathroom tells me I have been thinking wishfully. The house has been so badly damaged that it's not fit to occupy. Similarly, the bathrooms, which had been used as dumping grounds for the toxic chemicals employed in the cultivation of marijuana, are in my estimation, not fit for human use.

I clear from the scene with barely enough time to squeeze in a quick file follow-up. Last week I took a report of a shoplifting at a small convenience store. At that time, I'd made arrangements with the store owner to pick up surveillance footage on this evening. The store is supposed to close at 11:00 p.m. but I still have time to make it. I remember that the establishment was clean. Maybe they will let me use their bathroom.

10:59 p.m.
I make it to the convenience store with about a minute to spare before closing. The owner is in a rush and just wants to get home. He hands me the surveillance disk as he locks up. I don't have the heart to ask him to re-open just for me to use the facilities.

I settle once again into the familiar surroundings of my police vehicle and weigh my options. Since we have to "gear down," more so than our male counterparts in order to use the facilities, female members always know where the cleanest and least creepy bathrooms are in town. Unfortunately, I'm nowhere near any of those. The detachment is quite a ways away, but I decide it's my best bet. Of course it makes sense for me to fuel up my car on the way. I pull into the first gas station I see. Anyways, maybe they will have a reasonable bathroom.

11:23 p.m.
Bathroom fail. I should have known by the way the store clerk looked at me when he handed me the key that this bathroom would be worse than the one at the grow-op. After a quick survey of the toilet and sink, I turn around and walk right back out.

I rush to my car, reflecting with irony that both my vehicle and I now have "full tanks." Hopefully I can make it to the detachment before I get sent to another file. My dispatcher calls me on the radio. I sigh and accept the report she sends hopeful that I can still swing by the detachment on the way. I check the map and realize I've been sent as far as geographically possible from the detachment. I pull a U-turn.

11:37 p.m.
I attend the call: a dispute between neighbours. Two parties who have been unable to get along for the past fifteen years that they have lived side-by-side have picked tonight to call the police. I get both sides of the story. I cannot help but listen half-heartedly as each party complains about whose dog pooped on whose yard three years ago and which one's kids had six loud parties last month.

All I can do is think, "You people think you have problems?! I haven't used a bathroom since 5:30 p.m.!"

Despite my inward frustration, I manage to resolve the issue, at least for the night. In the interests of neutrality I choose not to ask either party to allow me a few minutes in their bathroom. Instead, I turn my vehicle towards the safe and familiar detachment. This is starting to get urgent.

12:21 a.m.

No sooner am I on the road, when one of the boys requests assistance. He has arrested a female and she needs to be searched incidental to arrest. Knowing I am the only female member working, I immediately respond. I acknowledge the request and advise that I am available to help my partner out. I ask where he wants to meet holding my breath and silently hoping he will say the detachment. He gives me the address. It is not the detachment.

1:12 a.m.

After the search, it gets busy. Very busy. Several important reports fill our dispatch queue and I pass through a drive-thru where I grab a very unhealthy lunch (but no drink) on my way to another file. No chance for me to take that bathroom break now. At least that urgent feeling has gone. I notice it tends to disappear after a few hours. Still, the dull pressure against my duty belt is a constant reminder that I really must visit a bathroom when I have a chance. At this point, almost anything will do. I start thinking about the disgusting bathrooms at the grow-op and gas station. Maybe I should have used one of those.

3:26 a.m.

A few hours and several files later, the night finally slows. That's when our Watch Commander reminds us that we are to set up a roadblock tonight.

The boys and I set up at a busy roadway and entrance point to our community. I look at my watch. It's now just about 10 hours since I last used the facilities. I eye the tree line several metres away. If only I were a boy and we were camping.

The driver of the third vehicle we stop smells like beer. He refuses to provide a sample of his breath which is a Criminal Code offence. Based on the circumstances of the file, he will be released at scene with paperwork compelling him to court. As I lean over the hood of my car to complete the paperwork, that urgent feeling comes rushing back. This is now an emergency and I decide that, no matter what, after I release this guy I will be ditching the roadblock and hitting the detachment.

I get about halfway through the paperwork and the guy starts complaining that he has to go to the bathroom.

I'm thinking, *Buddy, you have no idea.*

I tell him to relax and hold it (I certainly am!). But as I continue writing, he gets more and more insistent.

"I have to go NOW!" he shouts.

I write faster. The more he complains, the more I am reminded of my own situation. I am literally feeling his pain. I realize that the sooner I get the paper done, the sooner I can be on my way to the safe, clean bathroom waiting for me at the detachment. Oh, and this guy can go do whatever he needs to do as well. I tell him it will just be another minute or so and then he can be on his way (on foot of course).

His monotone response: "Too late."

I look up. He's already wet himself. I step over a spreading pool of urine genuinely shocked at the volume this guy had been holding. I briefly wonder if it would be worth it for me to follow suit. Yeah right. I shake my head and hand him his release paperwork. Then I add a few lines in my notebook about the incident before driving back to the detachment.

3:52 a.m.

I somehow manage to get back to the office without wetting myself. I barely make it through my pre-toilet hand washing ritual. My hands have been in all manner of filth all night and I always wash my hands before—as well as after—using the facilities. Of course, this practice now adds insult to injury. I hop from foot to foot as I rinse soap from my hands and then dance my way over to the stall, shedding kit along the way. In the stall, my duty belt hits the floor (no danger here). And finally... oh, blessed relief. And that's when dispatch calls.

"Delta One Three from Dispatch."

I groan. If I answer now, the telltale echo and sound of urination will alert every member in the city as to where I am. How embarrassing.

"Delta One Three from Dispatch," she repeats.

"Delta One Three is peeing!" I shout at the ceiling.

My work cell phone buzzes in my vest.

I sigh and rush through what had been the only moment of true "me time" on the shift thus far. After washing my hands, I respond on the radio while heading out the door.

"Sorry, Dispatch. I was having … radio issues. Were you calling Delta One Three?"

My dispatcher seems unconcerned about my unexplained absence. She probably knows where I was.

"Yes," she responds. "I need you to attend a file. A domestic assault. The complainant is specifically asking for a female member."

I look at my watch. Only about an hour left in the shift but it looks like I'll now be staying several hours later as a result of this new file. Maybe I should try and grab a coffee on the way.

THE SMALL RUNNING SHOE CAPER WITH BIG REWARDS
Sergeant Regina A. Marini

While on lone patrol on a cold wintry Saturday morning in Dauphin, Manitoba, I was dispatched to a chain department store for a shoplifting complaint. I headed directly to the store and spoke with the manager in his office. He told me that someone had stolen a pair of black winter boots right off the shelf.

"Let's go have a look," I suggested.

The manager walked me to the shoe department where I immediately noticed that someone had left a very dirty and well-worn pair of men's running shoes amongst the rows of factory-new black boots.

"Who do these belong to?" I asked.

The manager did not know.

I took a closer look. The shoes were quite worn and had holes in the soles. They were also very dirty and you could barely tell that they had been white at one time. Something was written along the midsole on the outside of each shoe. I couldn't believe my eyes. There, in faded black block letters, was written a first name and last initial. It was a first name and last initial that I recognized. I seized the shoes as evidence.

Of course, I knew the Boot Bandit and I knew where he lived. No less than a few weeks before, I had arrested him at a local hotel for fighting. The Boot Bandit was a very big man. He was at least 6'4-" and weighed about 300 lbs. That night, he'd been very intoxicated and had resisted arrest. It had taken three of us just to get him into the back seat of a police car. Once inside, he had promptly smashed one of the side windows with his feet. He had a reputation for being a fighter and for hating the police.

As it was Saturday morning, I figured the Boot Bandit likely had not yet had much time to get liquored up so I decided to go by his house. At the residence, I notified my dispatcher and I knocked at the front door.

"Come in," came the polite reply.

So I did. I immediately noticed several pairs of shoes at the front entrance. And there were those stolen black boots! And there he was. I found the Boot Bandit, sober and sitting in the kitchen with two other male friends. I thought how wonderful it would be if he were to put on those stolen boots. It would show he was claiming ownership of them and that he had likely stolen them.

I called him by name. "I have to talk to you privately. Do you mind coming outside and having a talk in my police car?"

To my surprise, he got up without argument, walked over to the entrance and put on those stolen boots. He followed me to my police car and climbed into the back seat. I told him how much I appreciated his cooperation. I remarked that the weather was getting really cold and commented about how essential it was to have good winter clothes and boots. He agreed.

I asked, "Where did you get those boots?"

His head slumped down and he groaned asking, "How did you know?"

Of course, I did not want the Boot Bandit to know that it had been his simple oversight of writing his name on his shoes that had given him away. I did, however, want to discourage him from stealing in the future so I warned him saying, "All the stores have cameras."

His head slumped even lower.

"I didn't know that," he said quietly.

I told the Boot Bandit that he was under arrest for theft and read him his rights. I then drove him back to the detachment to give him some court documents.

We got everyone's attention at the office when the giant Boot Bandit was escorted in by little 5'6-" me. I was the only female member at the detachment and several of my colleagues wanted to know not only why, but just how I'd managed to bring him in. My corporal could not believe that the Boot Bandit had written his name on his shoes, not to mention that he'd come along so peaceably when busted.

"Well that one goes in the record books," he laughed, shaking his head.

My early experience with the Boot Bandit taught me that catching people at the right time is just as important as catching them in the first place. Often, liquor can change a person's demeanour to such a degree that they are quite a different person from when they are sober. In the case of the Boot Bandit, dealing with him when he was sober and treating him with respect went a long way in solving this crime and also reducing the risk to my safety.

I will always remember the Boot Bandit and my "running shoe caper" with pride as a defining moment when I exceeded expectations, garnered some respect from colleagues and also affirmed my abilities as an effective police officer. The crime may have been small but the reward and return was immeasurable.

THE CITY SLICKER MEETS HER MATCH
Sergeant Mia Poscente

I like to consider myself adaptable, self-sufficient, and clever enough to maneuver through tricky and challenging situations. I have talked my way out of confrontations both as an undercover operator and as a uniformed police officer. With almost twenty years of policing experience, I have seen it all. Right? Not so fast. While some locals actually believe Toronto is the centre of the universe, I am at least open-minded enough to admit I could learn a thing or two and expand my experiences. That is precisely why an opportunity to work for a month in a remote, fly-in, First Nation reserve in Manitoba was so appealing to me.

I arrived by RCMP plane (I got to sit in the co-pilot seat!) in a rain storm, landing on a grass and gravel airstrip. Jack, the detachment commander, greeted me and led me to the waiting RCMP truck, then boat. With all my gear, I sat at the front of the boat and was pelted by ice as we bounced across Family Lake and through the channel to Little Grand Rapids, which would be my home until mid-October. It is much colder in Manitoba in September than it is in Toronto, and I questioned myself for volunteering to do this.

The next day was warmer, and after a crash course in driving the boat, Jack dropped the keys to the detachment in my hand and took off for his well-deserved vacation. Did I mention I had never driven a boat before? But really, how hard could it be? After all, it was a wide open body of water and there was nothing for me to hit.

I spent the next several weeks driving a truck and a quad, learning about life on a reserve and dealing with its unique policing challenges, all the while actively avoiding having to drive the boat. There were two boats, actually. The big boat (the one I learned to drive) had a one hundred and fifty-five engine (whatever that means), and the smaller boat had a ninety.

During my visit, the water levels had been dropping drastically and were apparently at the lowest levels ever seen by the locals. Rocks were sticking out of the water that had never even been mapped. At the RCMP dock on "the other side" (where we had to go to get mail, or go to the Northern Store, and airport) the water was less than a foot deep, making it extremely difficult to dock. One day, Evan, an experienced boater, grounded the ninety and had to get in the water to push it out while the rest of us sat in the boat, (he was the junior guy after all). The one hundred and fifty-five was too big and could no longer be used.

After a terrible snow storm (yes, in early October) that stranded several members both incoming and outgoing, we got up bright and early one Saturday morning to get everyone where they needed to be. Snow covered the boats as we prepared for the first of two trips across the lake. The sun was coming up and the intense autumn colours were made brilliant by the glistening frost. The lake was like glass; all remnants of the horrific storm winds were gone. Steam rose from the water in areas where the warmth of the sun touched down.

This was to be my day of reckoning: I had to drive the boat by myself back from the other side. As we got into the ninety for the first trip, Evan asked if I wanted to drive.

"No, you go ahead," I replied, not wanting to have to dock in the shallow water with witnesses.

Evan drove across the pristine water effortlessly and brought the boat to a smooth stop along the dock, facing out to make it easier for me to pull away. I retrieved the truck from the garage and drove Evan and the others to the airport, returning to the dock alone.

"It's just you and me," I said aloud to myself as I started the boat engine.

I had watched closely as other members pulled out from dock, so I knew what to do. I dropped the engine very slowly as I crept away from the dock. Once away from the rocks and into deeper water, I dropped it a bit more and pushed down on the throttle. The nose of the boat went up, as expected, and I repeated what Jack had told me in my boat-driving lesson a month earlier.

"Turn the steering wheel back and forth to bring the nose down then open 'er up. If the nose doesn't come down, trim up," was what Jack had said.

Prior to this I thought "trim" was what you did with your hair when it was a bit too long. But now I knew it was also a reference to raising or lowering the outboard motor on a boat. Look at me using lingo!

I opened 'er up and the nose went up, so I trimmed up, then the nose went up some more, so I turned the wheel back and forth, but the nose didn't come down. I couldn't see the water over the front of the boat, except when I smashed down onto it. Over and over, up in the air with the engine roaring so loud I could actually hear it echoing off the distant trees. Then SMASH down onto the water, then RRRNNNMMM up in the air—my feet came off the deck and as I held onto the steering wheel I felt like a flag waving in the wind.

Don't let gooooooooo! I screamed in my head, unable to reach the throttle to slow down.

I bounced the boat off the water about ten times before the engine finally conked out and I drifted to a stop in a circle of wake. Further out, the water remained like glass and I became perplexed by how calm the water was out there, yet how rough it was where I was driving. I remained calm by reminding myself that it was fresh water and there were no sharks.

"Okay," I said to myself, "remember what Jack said: 'Put it in neutral, start the engine and get going again.'"

I did, and it worked. So I started cutting through the water again. Up came the nose and I turned the steering wheel back and forth, and I trimmed up, and I opened 'er up and RRRNNNMMM—SPLASH—RRRNNNMMM—SPLASH, over and over and again and again, all the way across the lake. I came through the channel toward our dock doing a wheelie with the boat, and as I slowed down, a huge wake I had caused swept past the boat, swamping the dock where the remaining three people stood in silence, awestruck no doubt by the spectacle before them. I carefully docked the boat and stepped out, doing my best to conceal my shaking legs, as someone took the rope and tied it off. Together, and in complete silence, we loaded up and all got back in the boat.

"Want me to drive?" George suggested quietly.

"Sure," I replied.

And in complete silence he drove across the pristine water effortlessly, and brought the boat to a smooth stop along the dock, facing out to make it easier for me to pull away.

Still without a word spoken, we all got out of the boat and loaded everything onto the truck. There wasn't room for all of us in the cab, so two of us would have to ride in the back. I hopped into the truck bed, as did Ann-Marie, with whom I had become good friends. As the truck doors closed and we were out of hearing from the others, she broke the silence by turning to me and demanded, "What the hell was that?"

Having as close to a complete meltdown as I have ever had in my life, I sobbed, "I couldn't get the nose down on the boat!"

"No kidding," she chided. "We could hear you from across the frickin' lake! You came around the corner like this..." Anne-Marie motioned with her hand almost straight up in the air. "What were you doing?"

"Jack said to trim up to get the nose down!" I pleaded in my defence.

"On the one-fifty-five! On the ninety you have to trim *down* to get the nose down!" she said with exasperation.

"How was I supposed to know that?" I cried.

"Well it's all over now," she consoled me. "Pull yourself together and whatever you do, just don't show weakness to the guys!"

With that we had a good laugh and I realized I was not as rugged as I thought I was. I could laugh at myself and with my friends. This would be one of those stories that I would tell over and over again. But, unlike "the fish that got away," I wouldn't have to embellish because there were witnesses.

Order up the "I survived a month in Little Grand Rapids" t-shirt and get me back home!

ZERO AVENUE
Corporal Donna Morse, née Burns (Ret.)

It had been a warm August night in Surrey, British Columbia and I was just approaching the final 60 minutes of my 12 hour night shift. Heading back to the detachment, I took Zero Avenue, which ran parallel to the Canada-United States border. This put me in the perfect place at the right moment to take the next file that came in.

I was dispatched to speak with a distraught male at a small convenience store located close to the Pacific Highway Border Crossing. I found the man outside the store. The 30-year-old was very agitated and refused to speak with me. Pacing back and forth, he took long drags on a cigarette. He was bare-chested and had multiple scratches on his upper torso. I noticed dried blood on his jeans.

I had no idea as to what had happened to this man or why he was so visibly upset and disheveled. I did my best to calm him down as I knew he would not give me any information in his agitated state. After finishing his cigarette, the male seemed a bit more calm but still was not helpful in telling me what had happened. All he would say was that his car had been stolen. I coaxed him for further information while trying to keep him focused on remaining calm. After a few minutes, he disclosed that he had left his red Honda Civic a ways up the highway, but that when he arrived back at the location where he had parked, he'd found his vehicle was gone. This did not seem right. Why would he have left his vehicle at the side of the road in such a rural area? What was he doing out on Zero Avenue at this early hour? And then there was the blood. Was the male a victim, or had he done something bad? I needed more information.

I was able to convince the male to get into my police vehicle and he joined me as I drove up the highway searching for the missing car. We found it a few blocks north of the convenience store. It was in reasonable condition and did not look stolen.

Suddenly, the male became even more disturbed, telling me that his three-year-old son was missing. He said the kid must have been taken from the vehicle when it was stolen. The male became uncooperative when I asked further questions. I had no way of telling whether the story of the three-year-old was fact or fiction, but I was now concerned for the welfare of a child.

While I continued trying to get further information from the man, my dispatcher notified me that a police officer from the neighbouring American town of Blaine, Washington wanted to speak with me. Arrangements were made for me to meet the Blaine police officer in Canada Customs at the nearby Pacific Highway Border Crossing. With the male still in my police vehicle, I headed to the border.

I escorted the male into Canada Customs and got him to sit in the waiting area. He was still extremely distressed and kept stating that his child was missing, but when I asked for further details, he refused to answer. However, as it turned out, my trip to the border gave me another piece of the puzzle. I spoke with the Blaine police officer who had asked me to meet him along with some US Border agents.

The US Border agents filled me in, telling me that my male had crossed into the United States in the early hours that morning. The male had arrived at the border in a red Honda Civic, stating that he was heading to Seattle to pick up his girlfriend. Although there had been no grounds to deny him entry into the United States, something had not felt right so the US Border agents had alerted the Blaine Police Department who dispatched a police officer to follow the male into town.

The Blaine police officer continued recounting the story, advising that he had followed the male through the town and observed him stop on a bridge spanning a small river. It had appeared to the police officer that the male had removed something from his car and thrown it over the railing into the water. But when the police officer stopped and questioned the male, he could find no evidence of wrongdoing and an immediate search of the river produced nothing out of the ordinary. Due to the male's suspicious behaviour, the Blaine police officer had decided to escort him back to the border for immediate re-entry into Canada.

The US Border agents confirmed that there was no record of a young boy having been in the vehicle upon entry to the United States, but the agent who dealt directly with the male told me that he had seen a rolled up blanket in the back seat. Could the three-year-old have been wrapped in this blanket? Was the blanket what the police officer had observed being thrown into the river in Blaine? But the Blaine police officer was adamant that the river had been thoroughly checked. It was shallow and there was absolutely no way a blanket, or a body, could have been missed.

While I was still sorting through the information from the US Border agents and the Blaine police officer, officials from the Peace Arch Border Crossing, located several kilometres west of us, called concerning a woman being held at US Immigration. The woman had been questioned at the border when she tried to cross into Canada and held for investigation when her story seemed off. The woman was reporting that she was a resident of Seattle and that her Canadian boyfriend was supposed to have picked her up earlier that morning. When her boyfriend had not shown up, the woman had ultimately decided to make her own way to the border. She claimed that she did not know of her boyfriend having a child and had no idea why he had not picked her up. Things were getting very confusing, but my main focus at that point was determining whether or not there was a missing child and then finding him if he did exist.

After much coaxing, I managed to get the phone number for the man's mother and phoned her. She turned out to be just as helpful as her son. She confirmed that the male had weekend custody of her three-year-old grandson but refused to give me any information about who the mother was. She did, however, give me the address of where her son resided in Vancouver. I radioed my dispatcher and asked her to contact the Vancouver Police Department to have them to check it out.

Something about this file was not right.

When members of the Vancouver Police Department arrived at the male's address, they found the body of a female in the alleyway directly behind the house. I knew the male had not been truthful with me and had been withholding information the entire time I had been dealing with him. And now there was a body in the alleyway behind his house. I made the decision to arrest him for obstruction.

I took him to Surrey Detachment and arranged to have his car towed to the police compound. At the detachment, he was interviewed and his jeans were seized in relation to the body in the alleyway.

After a few hours, he finally confessed.

We learned that he had indeed been planning to pick up his girlfriend in Seattle that morning. Realizing that he would not be allowed to take his son into the United States, he decided to improvise. He had dropped his three-year-old son in the woods just north of the border so that he could drive down to Seattle alone and collect his girlfriend. Unfortunately, when he returned, he realized he could not remember precisely where he had left his son. He scraped up his upper torso while franticly searching the underbrush.

The confession initiated a search involving several agencies. Emergency services personnel located the little boy along with the blanket and flashlight his father had left with him. We were all relieved to find him alive after 36 hours. Ultimately, the father was convicted on a variety of charges relating to the care and wellbeing of his son.

We were never able to get an explanation about what it was that was dropped off that bridge in Blaine. But believe it or not, the body found behind the male's house was just a strange coincidence and had nothing to do with my file.

I have thought of that young boy many times over the years. I sincerely hope that he's living a good and fulfilling life and that he has no memory of that traumatic experience almost thirty years ago.

PRIME DUST UP
Constable Tammy Um

In 2003, I served as the Drum Major for the RCMP Cadet Band at Depot. Every day, band members scarfed down lunch and grabbed their instruments to perform the noon parade. In my case, I did not grab an instrument, I took the Drum Major's staff.

Though there was often a crowd of hundreds of civilian spectators, the drill staff did not hold back their feelings about performances. They often screamed at me from across the parade square if I made a mistake. Over time, the fear and uncertainty that my band mates and I experienced started to fade away. "It's just words," we would tell each other. We quickly learned to harden ourselves against harsh public criticism.

Fast forward to 2009.

Excuse me, I thought. *Did I want to what!?*

Literally two minutes earlier I had been directly responsible for the life of the Prime Minister as he slept in the Explorer Hotel in Iqaluit, Nunavut. Now, having stepped out for some fresh air, I was being propositioned by a drunk on the street. And "propositioned" is classing it up.

August in Iqaluit means that it is still sunny at night and, as such, a huge shadow was cast by this towering, intoxicated man who had gotten right in my face with his vulgar offer.

When we protect the Prime Minister, we typically are not in uniform. We are supposed to fade into the background, only appearing if there is a problem. Clearly this man did not realize that the sharply dressed women he had found walking out of the hotel at night was an on-duty, fully prepared, police officer. I thought telling him would immediately diffuse the situation. Nope, he did not care.

Using every vulgarity he had the first time, and with absolutely no volume control, he made his offer again.

With two fully indecent offers on the table and the Prime Minister sleeping just a few meters away, I decided to arrest the man for disturbing the peace. I figured I could whisk him away from the hotel without incident. Nope, again. In fact, he actually said, "nope" as he turned to run away.

I grabbed the drunk's collar and he spun towards me. I knew that in a straight on punching match, I was going to lose. So, as I was not sure of his intentions, I simply spun him around by pushing on one shoulder and pulling on the other so that I was presented with his back. My arm snaked around his throat and I secured him in a pseudo chokehold. Suddenly, he noodled and collapsed on the ground in front of me. I knelt, handcuffed him and radioed the members working in uniform to come and pick him up. They were there in a jiffy, especially as the landmark Iqaluit Detachment on Astro Hill was right next door.

What I had not known was that early into the incident, two bouncers had come running to my assistance when they'd heard the man yelling sexual obscenities at me. But they had stopped short and watched as I efficiently and professionally took control of the situation and the man. They had been floored that a female officer could actually down someone easily twice her size!

One of the bouncers was also a dispatcher for the Fire Department. I became Fire Hall legend for a short while. The bouncers managed to get a copy of the surveillance tape and played my takedown as proof of their story.

Before my RCMP experience, I would have gone to pieces if a stranger had approached me on the street in the middle of the "night" like this guy did. Who would have figured that becoming the tough little ninja that I am today would have started by joining a band?

I'm only five foot three, but I'm a Member of the Royal Canadian Mounted Police! I march in bands, I protect the Prime Minister while he sleeps and I, like the thousands of other females in the RCMP, walk tall and get the job done across the globe. Represent!

STANDOFF
Constable Constance Henderson

I was born in Surrey, British Columbia and spent the first two decades of my life in the Lower Mainland. I graduated from Depot and became a Mountie in the spring of 2007. One week later, I worked my first shift in Northern Alberta at Desmarais Detachment. Although Desmarais is the official RCMP name for the posting, the locals there commonly refer to the area as The Hamlet of Wabasca. When I started working there, I was the only female member to have been posted to the detachment in the preceding three years. There were no movie theatres, no sushi restaurants and no malls. Desmarais was certainly very different from Surrey.

I was not supposed to be working in Desmarais. It was my regular day off and I was actually scheduled for an overtime shift that evening in Slave Lake. I had taken the shift to allow the members at the neighbouring detachment a chance to enjoy their annual Christmas party. Because I had known I would be working a night shift, I had stayed up late the night before, going to bed at around 4:00 a.m. In order to allow my body to adjust to staying awake during nightshifts, I had learned to stay up very late the night before, try to sleep straight through the morning, and then, after getting up in the late afternoon, do a few things around the house before my shift started for the evening. This strategy sometimes worked, and I would end up with a solid eight to twelve hours of sleep before starting nights. But sometimes, this was not the case.

Desmarais was a small posting and we had limited assets. There were just eight constables who were supervised by one corporal and one sergeant. If another member got sick or had to leave the area on a file, I would sometimes be called to work with no notice. I was also often on call. This meant that while I would be free on a day off to do groceries or housework, I could never stray far from home. Once the phone rang, I would have to immediately drop everything and head in to work.

Just after 7:00 a.m., I awoke to the sound of loud knocking at my front door. I shared my residence, (a two level, 1,000 square foot, four bedroom house that seemed to be about 200 years old), with three male members who also worked at my detachment. None of them seemed to be answering the door. Finally, I stumbled out of bed and found my way to the front door, still half asleep. I opened the door to find one of my on-duty coworkers standing on the front step. He was in uniform. If he noticed my semiconscious state, he did not say anything about it. Instead, he asked me if my roommates were home.

I checked the basement, but none of the guys were around. I asked what was up. My coworker told me that he was heading out on a file and was hoping to get some backup. The area where he was headed was well known to the members at our detachment. Radio signals were spotty and there was zero cell phone coverage, so when possible, members attended the area in pairs. But on that date when there were no on-duty members available to assist my coworker, he would come to my house looking for backup.

My coworker told me a bit about the file. He was going to deal with a mentally unstable man who was in crisis and had not slept in three days. The male's frightened family members had just called the detachment saying that he was now outside the family residence behaving erratically. He was also holding a gun.

I obviously would not let my coworker go to such a file by himself, so I got dressed into my uniform and hopped into the police truck as his partner. We radioed our dispatcher and let her know where we were going. We all knew the issues in the geographical area. Radio coverage would be spotty and our cell phones would most definitely be completely useless.

My partner and I drove for about 20 minutes over paved and then gravel roads. Our dispatcher, who was communicating over the phone with the family, told us that the suspect was still in the driveway. He had put the gun down on the ground between a pickup truck and a jeep but had reportedly filled a backpack with various weapons that oddly included a set of nunchucks.

When my partner and I finally arrived at the house, we saw the male standing at the end of the driveway. He was wearing a backpack. When he saw us, he started yelling at us. It was very difficult to understand him, but from what we were able to make out, it was clear that he hated cops. Of course being dressed as we were in police uniforms and having arrived to the scene in a marked police vehicle made it quite clear to the man that my partner and I were indeed cops. He began cursing and threatening us.

My partner and I had a job to do and we certainly couldn't effectively reason with the male from the front seat of the police truck, so we got out to approach him. But as soon as my boots hit the ground, the male turned around and began running back up the driveway towards the house. My partner and I began chasing him were unable to reach him before he managed to grab the gun from between the pickup truck and the jeep. It was a long barreled black gun.

"Gun!" I shouted, and dove behind a second pickup truck that was parked on the property. This truck had no wheels and I was worried that it also might not have an engine block, but it was better than nothing. I remember literally flying through the air as I dove for cover. My partner followed right behind me.

I could not see much from behind the cover of the derelict truck. My view of the man was obstructed as he had now ducked down between the first pickup truck and jeep. I noticed as I peeked out, looking down the barrel of my pistol, that there was a dog in the bed of the first pickup truck. It was stressed out and pacing around. This constant movement made it difficult for me to determine the man's exact location. But my partner, from where he was positioned on the other end of the derelict truck, had a clear view.

My partner shouted, "Put the gun down! Put the gun down!"

The man did not comply. I then heard the unmistakable sound of a long gun being loaded. I was suddenly very afraid.

"He's loading it," I warned my partner.

"He's pointing it at us," my partner informed me.

My fingers were going numb around the grip of my pistol. It might have been because it was minus 15 degrees Celsius, or it might have been because of what my partner had just said.

Looking beyond the first pickup truck and jeep I saw at least six silhouettes in the large bay window of the family residence. These six people, who were now watching our drama unfold on their front lawn, had called police because they had been worried about their nephew. I was sure they had not called expecting us to shoot him. Let's be clear: The male was pointing a loaded firearm at police. We were justified to use lethal force in order to save our lives and those of his family. But how would they react if that's what we did? They certainly wouldn't praise us. But would they turn on us? Would there be more people with guns to deal with? All of these thoughts rushed through my mind in an instant.

Meanwhile, my partner continued telling the male to drop his gun. The male did not comply and instead instructed my partner to put *his* gun down. Then, he suddenly tucked his gun between his back and the backpack and ran to a neighbouring house which we later learned belonged to a member of his extended family. We had the family from the first house call the resident of the second house and tell him to leave. We told everyone to stay inside the first house and away from the windows. Now the suspect was the only person remaining inside the second house. He barricaded himself inside along with the long gun and backpack full of weapons. My partner and I took up positions around the house.

While all of this had been going on, our dispatcher had been dutifully trying to check on us via radio. Of course, as it turned out, the spot our suspect had picked for his standoff had been particularly bad for radio coverage. During the incident, we had had no way to update our dispatcher. That had been a very lonely feeling. Now, neither my partner nor I could leave our positions at the second residence in order to search for a viable location to send or receive a radio transmission. We also had no way of getting a message to the family in the first house to call the detachment on our behalf and I actually was not convinced they would be overly helpful even if we asked. We had no way to communicate with dispatch.

Our dispatcher, who was quite switched on, had already sent another Mountie up to check on us in person. Our sergeant arrived at the scene and we discussed the situation, agreeing that there were two options: we could wait four hours for the Regional Emergency Response Team to arrive from Edmonton, or we could, as my sergeant put it, "storm it" right then and there. We opted for the latter.

My sergeant kicked in the front door. The suspect was located in the living room, watching TV in his underwear. He was promptly placed under arrest. I then drove him four hours to the nearest hospital where he could be treated for his mental health issues.

At the hospital, I escorted him into the admitting area. He sat, handcuffed, on a bench while I dealt with the charge nurse. I was asked why I had brought the male in and what made me think he should be admitted.

I made a point of looking at my watch as I said, "Oh, about four hours ago, he had a gun pointed at me."

The charge nurse called for security.

I slept a few hours at Alberta K Division Headquarters in Edmonton and then drove four hours from Edmonton to Slave Lake where I worked a 10 hour night shift so that the members there could enjoy their well-deserved Christmas party. It was a busy night. But that's another story.

THAILAND
Staff Sergeant Nav Hothi

On December 26, 2004 I awoke, belly still full of Christmas turkey, to a world in shock. On every news channel there was extensive coverage of the 2004 Indian Ocean earthquake and subsequent tsunami. The images of the damage and loss of life were horrific. The 9.1 magnitude earthquake had caused a tsunami which had wiped out 220,000 people and many more were reported missing. I watched the footage in my parents' living room, half a world away from the devastation. I had no idea that I would soon become part of the humanitarian response.

At the time, I was serving as a member of the RCMP Forensic Identification Section (FIS) in the Lower Mainland of British Columbia. My job was to analyze crime scenes, determine cause of death and identify human remains. Like all RCMP forensic specialists I had undergone a rigorous training program which included a two month classroom based course, a ten month field training program and a final oral board examination. The RCMP FIS training was, and remains today, world renowned and RCMP forensic specialists have an international reputation as being some of the best fingerprint examiners in the world. It should therefore not have been a surprise to find the email in my inbox upon my return to work.

The RCMP Forensic Identification Section Program Director was canvassing for FIS members willing to deploy to Thailand to assist with disaster victim identification. Many Canadians had been reported missing in the busy tourist area of Phuket, Thailand and the Government of Canada had requested that the RCMP assist in victim repatriation. The email created a bit of a buzz in the FIS office. There was discussion of the risks to health and safety posed by Thailand's damaged infrastructure. We were all aware of the guaranteed hazardous working conditions and the likelihood of exposure to disease. These were valid concerns but I knew I had to go and help in any way I could. I replied as quickly as my fingers could type, telling my program director that I was available for deployment at the drop of a hat.

On the morning of January 1, 2005, I awoke to the sound of my phone ringing. I fumbled for the cell, still groggy from my late night ringing in the New Year. On the other end of the line was my supervisor. At first I thought there might have been a murder overnight which would require my attendance somewhere local. But instead, through my daze, I heard him ask if I could be on a plane to Ottawa that evening. That woke me up pretty quickly. And I said yes.

I sprang into action and within six hours had packed what I thought I needed for my trip, (how does one prepare for something like this?), booked a flight, located my passport and was on my way to Ottawa along with three other FIS specialists from my Division.

In Ottawa, a team of RCMP FIS specialists from across the country had been assembled. Our first order of business was to get immunized. Fortunately for me, I'd taken a trip to Africa during the previous year which meant that most of my immunizations were up to date. But some of my colleagues were "poked" many times. Our bags were filled with the anti-malarials and antibiotics we would need to take during our stay overseas. Then, the stores for International Deployment were opened and our team was issued mosquito netting, sleeping bags, first aid kits (the suture kit worried me), water purification tablets, flashlights and everything we could possibly need for deployment where the infrastructure was damaged. I started to get nervous and excited at the same time.

The next day, we headed to the airport to board our flight to Bangkok. The team—ten of us in total—really had no idea what to expect. This was the first time most of us had worked outside of the country, and in a non-investigational role at that. Although we knew our job was to identify victim remains, we did not know with whom we would be working, where in Phuket we would be assigned, or what our work and living arrangements would be.

When we got to the airport, we realized the uniqueness of the situation. We were met by CBC reporters and I soon had a microphone and camera shoved into my face. In my regular job back home, I would have been able to simply direct the enquiries to the designated RCMP media liaison officer. But in this case, things were different so I answered what questions I could. Family and friends said we looked both excited and nervous. I never watched the footage.

Twenty hours later, we arrived in Phuket, Thailand. Having visited the country a few years earlier on vacation, I was excited to be in Thailand again. But I was well aware that this time it was not a tourist trip. We were there to work and I was eager to get to the task at hand. Multiple morgues had been set up in the country. We were assigned to the one in the town of Krabi. This morgue contained the remains of many tourists and locals from neighbouring islands, including Koh Phi Phi, an idyllic island in the middle of the Andaman Sea. We believed that the remains of many Canadians reported missing would be located at this morgue.

Fortunately, the beach town of Krabi had not been damaged by the tsunami so much of the infrastructure remained intact. Our fears of insufficient housing and access to food and water had been unfounded, though we knew our colleagues working in various other communities were not so lucky. My team was housed in a hotel that was comfortable and efficient and close to our worksite. The mosquito netting and sleeping bags had probably been overkill, but I was glad that we'd been properly prepared. We settled into our hotel and prepared our gear for the next day.

Working with human remains has never made me feel uncomfortable. My experience working in hospitals prior to joining the RCMP taught me about the realities of death. I also believed I was a seasoned forensic specialist. I had been to countless hospital morgues, examined an untold number of bodies and participated in numerous autopsies. I'd even once observed two autopsies conducted in tandem. So I could handle the task at hand, right? The first day of work in Krabi was an eye opener. The team had been assigned a local driver whose job was to shuttle us where we needed to go. On our first day of work, he drove us up to a Buddhist temple. This was our temporary morgue. The spirituality of the location was not lost on me and seemed strangely appropriate. As I walked in, I noticed large refrigeration trailers lining both sides of the entryway and leading into the main plaza. There were over 15 trailers, all containing human remains. Then my eyes fixed on a wall of coffins. The temple was crammed with row upon row of wooden coffins, stacked five high. I felt my pulse quicken as in an instant, the gravity and enormity of the tragedy struck me. This was unlike any morgue I had ever been in.

Unfortunately, there was no time to recognize and reflect on the tragedy of events. We had a job to do. We soon discovered that the morgue had not been run efficiently prior to our arrival. Several different teams from all over the world had been doing their best to work side-by-side. There was a de facto lead team, but there was no agreement in policy or procedure which had impacted productivity. There were also cultural procedures that created delays. Out of respect for local customs, the morgue was not opened until prayers were completed by a monk each day. Unfortunately the monk was sometimes delayed until midday which meant that precious hours of daylight were lost.

In typical Canadian fashion, we had humbly assumed we had be the least experienced and capable team. The other teams had the opportunity to train in Disaster Victim Identification and work together on a regular basis whereas our team was made up of members from all across Canada who had just met days before. But, in keeping with our Mountie legacy, we proved capable of pulling together to get the job done. In fact, our team's arrival was welcomed, almost heralded. As the leader of another team told us: "We have been waiting for the RCMP to arrive. We know you will sort everything out."

Recognizing how important it was to respect local customs, we all worked with the local officials and the team leaders had a delicate discussion with the monk. We explained the necessity of starting work as early as possible to maximize the use of daylight, especially as electrical lighting in the temple was so poor. The monk understood, and the next day the process changed. From then on, a group of local women showed up promptly at 8:00 a.m. every day to recite the prayers for the dead.

Meanwhile, we got down to work. To improve efficiency, individual members of our team were embedded into the teams already working in the morgue. I had the opportunity to work with a team of dentists, taking and developing X-rays of teeth to be compared against available dental records. After a brief training session, I became a dental X-ray technician. I learned the difference between a bitewing and a periapical X-ray. My dentist at home is always impressed.

The working conditions were nothing like we were used to. We worked under tents in the temple courtyard on regular tables which were covered with garbage bags each morning. The only running water came from a single tap on the wall and electricity was unreliable due to frequent power outages. There was one rustic toilet for all the staff to share. The equipment was very basic and disease management consisted of members of the military spraying DDT on the concrete floors. The floors, which got quite dirty, were rinsed at the end of the day. As one can imagine, the stench was sometimes unbearable.

We worked at a very fast pace. There was no walking from table to table. It was a sprint. We hardly ever stopped for lunch, and then only if the food was brought to us. We worked long hours with no days off. It was over 40 degrees Celsius with high humidity during our stay. I would pull off my rubber boots at the end each day and pour about a cup of sweat out of each boot. Both the conditions and the work were challenging, but we also found what we were doing to be rewarding. We were giving families closure.

It was not just what I did as a humanitarian aid worker that impacted me, it was also what I saw. I was awed to see how such an affected community could come together and move forward. Local businesses would donate food that volunteers would prepare outside the morgue to feed and nourish the family members congregating each day awaiting word of their missing loved ones. There were volunteers who came in droves to do whatever they could to help: A Belgium hiker who transported remains to the morgue; a Thai doctor who would finish her graveyard shifts at a local hospital and then come straight to the morgue to work another eight hours; the foreign residents from the nearby islands who simply wanted to help in any capacity, whether that be in the morgue or outside at the communal kitchen. For me, it was an experience of immense growth in human understanding and compassion to witness and be part of such an impactful group of people.

The RCMP team was in Thailand for twenty-four days. I found the return to Canada to be as jarring as my departure. We were sent to Ottawa for a day of debriefings prior to returning home. When

I returned to my community, I was overwhelmed by well-meaning friends and family wanting to hear of my experiences. Colleagues and co-workers were fascinated by the work and processes. The local media wanted interviews. Processing the experience—the shocking, the good, the witness of hope—took a lot of time, years almost. Even ten years later, the experience remains as an indelible mark on my psyche. It was something that changed me for the better.

Constable Aaron Sheedy hails from Orillia, Ontario, and joined the RCMP after a career in outdoor education. He was posted to the Toronto Airport Detachment out of Depot, and has spent the last nine years investigating drug importations and corruption at the Lester B. Pearson International Airport. In addition to Aaron's daily policing duties, he is also a Narcotics Detector-Dog Handler and a member of the Ontario Tactical Troop. Aaron's policing duties have taken him from sea to sea in Canada, plus the Arctic.

Aaron draws from his policing experiences, the people he meets, his travels, and the natural world to write fiction and non-fiction with a predominately Canadian bent. Aaron lives and writes in Caledon, Ontario, Canada.

Corporal Veronica Fox was born and raised in the Lower Mainland of British Columbia. Veronica started a career path in journalism but switched streams to focus on policing after some positive experiences volunteering for a local police department. She worked as a 9-1-1 call taker for a number of years before being accepted by the RCMP. After graduating from Depot, she was posted to General Duty at Richmond Detachment in British Columbia where she had the opportunity to gain experience in

Media and Youth Investigation and where she also discovered a passion for Marine Patrol. Veronica now works with high risk offenders as a member of the Behavioural Sciences Group at Headquarters in British Columbia. Veronica holds a Bachelor of Arts in Communication and Sociology from Simon Fraser University and a Master of Arts in Leadership from Royal Roads University. She enjoys writing and was a contributor to the first publication of Red Coat Diaries: True Stories from the Royal Canadian Mounted Police. In her time off-duty Veronica enjoys hiking, cooking and teaching criminology.

Sergeant Regina Marini has been a Mountie for over thirty years. From postings in Manitoba and Ontario she has performed the full gambit of policing duties including Highway Patrol, Financial Crime, high level Securities Fraud and major event planning (i.e. Toronto's G20). She holds a Law Degree from Carleton University as well as numerous policing related certificates and citations including "Long Service" and "Service With Distinction" awards. Stemming from her wide policing experience and  education she is a sought after lecturer, having lectured across Canada and internationally. Currently she teaches College level Justice Studies courses and is the Professional Development Director for the Ontario Women in Law Enforcement. Add to all of this, she holds the very important roles of wife and mother to a busy hockey family. When time allows Regina can be found reading, gardening and spending time with her two much loved dogs ... if she isn't roaring down the road on her motorcycle.